Before We Tie The Knot

Before We
Tie The Knot

A handbook for the soon to be
or recently wed couple.

by

Dave Powers

Harvest Publishing
Newport Beach, California

Before We Tie The Knot
Copyright 2007 by Dave Powers
ISBN 978-0-6151-7811-0

Harvest Publishing, Newport Beach,California

Dedicated to the couples who took the biggest step of their lives and trusted me to be a part of the journey.

Contents

Introduction

In the past year, over a million couples have stood before a pastor, a justice of the peace, or a judge and committed themselves to each other in matrimony. Studies indicate there are more than two-million additional couples in the U.S. who are thinking and planning to do the same. For the vast majority their wedding day is something they have given a lot of thought and preparation to. The hope shared by all of these couples is their wedding day would fulfill the hopes and expectations they have for that day.

Before We Tie The Knot addresses several of the key issues couples will be facing. It is not a complete treatise on all aspects of matrimony. But it does give couples some things to think about, things that may have gone unnoticed. The author sets out to help couples get everything out of their wedding day and their marriage they had hoped for. By providing some insights from thirty-seven years as a pastor, counseling couples, conducting their wedding ceremonies and watching some of the good and not so good decisions couples have made along the way.

So get a cup of coffee, find a comfortable chair, get a note pad and sit down with a pastor that loves to talk with couples about marriage and making the most of their wedding day.

Chapter One

Start At The End

The couple sitting across the desk from me where filled with anticipation. They were ready to talk about their wedding day. So we began as I had done hundreds of times before, "Where do you see your relationship going? What will it look like in five years, in ten years, in twenty years?" The couple didn't really have an answer. That wasn't what they expected, I mean really, who thinks about the next twenty years when you're just trying to make it through the next two months with all that needs to be done just to get married? But this really is a question worth asking, "What do we want out of our marriage?"

A number of years ago, Dr Nick Stinett of the University of Nebraska supervised a study of families, hundreds of families. These were families that demonstrated a healthy balance of happiness and satisfaction. He found several consistent characteristics of a close knit healthy family:
1. A high degree of appreciation for each other
2. A great deal of time spent together
3. Good communication practices
4. A strong sense of commitment to the family unit
5. A deep-felt religious belief
6. An ability to deal with crisis in a positive manner

When we look at this list we find some of the same key issues the Bible addresses. A deeper investigation into the Bible reveals that on three separate occasions Jesus taught specifically on marriage, the Apostle Paul devotes an entire chapter to marriage and on sixteen separate occasions the New Testament writers give specific instruction about how to have a healthy marriage. That's really what we're looking for in a marriage, not a perfect marriage, just a healthy marriage. Quite often we may hear someone say they just want a *normal* marriage, or perhaps just a normal family. We usually hear this when a family or a couple has been under a lot of stress or going through some tough times, "I wish we just had a normal family."

But guess what normal is? A normal marriage in this country has a 50/50 chance of not ending in a divorce. A normal marriage in this country has a 1 in 3 chance of exercising some form of overt hostility, a physical abuse to one of the marriage partners. A normal marriage will often have prolonged periods of loud arguments, or fits of anger or days of isolating silence. With that "normality" in mind, we need to ask, "Do we really want a normal, average, American marriage?"

When I address this issue with a couple and then explain the difference between a normal marriage and a healthy marriage, without exception couples are quick to say, "Well of course we want a healthy marriage!" So let's get a working definition of a healthy marriage. *A healthy marriage is two people taking individual responsibility for nurturing the relationship they share together.* That definition can also apply between parent/child, between family members, even between friends. When we set out to work on a healthy marriage, there are at least four essential ingredients every healthy marriage needs.

In Matthew 19:5 Jesus taught, *"For this reason a man will leave his father and mother and be united to his wife, and the two will become one flesh? So they are no longer two, but one. Therefore what God has joined together, let man not separate."* In these few words Jesus addresses the issue of security. Every married couple needs to know father & mother have been left, and the two are now building a marriage, a family together. This is sometimes a difficult issue for couples, especially if one of the two has been very close to or dependent on their father or mother. God understands our need for security. For without security, the confidence of our partner is compromised. So when stress comes on the relationship, and there will be stress in every relationship, the power to resolve is compromised because of the suspicion that mom & dad are still part of the equation. In fact it can leave us feeling stuck in the middle.

Several years ago I was conducting the wedding rehearsal for a young couple. We had talked several times in our counseling sessions about the control both of their mothers had exercised in their homes as they grew up. Their moms were not bad, evil mothers, they just had powerful personalities. And their influence showed up at the wedding rehearsal.

Things had been going pretty good, we were just about to finish the rehearsal, when I looked in the front pew of the sanctuary and there sat the bride, sobbing. Being the ever observant pastor, I sat down and asked, "Is everything OK?" (Notice the great diplomacy?) To which the bride lifted her head from her hands, with tears streaming down her face and responded, "No! Everything I'm doing is not OK! My mom wants this, his mom wants that. Nobody is the least bit interested in what I want!" So I asked, "Which would you like to do?" "Neither!!" she replied. Whereupon she explained to me exactly what she would wanted in her wedding ceremony. I then took her by the hand, looked at her with a smile and told her, "Then that's what we will do." "We will? Who's going to tell our mothers?" the bride asked. "I will that's why you pay me the five dollars." was my response.

So I stood before the wedding party, explained the changes we were making and here comes the moms! Marching right down the middle aisle, red faces in immediate disapproval. "Who said we're doing that?" was their demand. "I said" was my response. "I out weigh both of you by a good twenty pounds and this is the way we're going to do this ceremony!" To the grooms credit, he stood his ground and faced both of "the controlling moms" and the bride watched as her future husband stood in the gap and took the heat from two very influential people in their lives. They both learned a lesson in security that evening.

One of the key ingredients of security is trust. With no trust a marriage will not last because there is no security in the relationship. This is why it is so important in the early stages of a marriage to keep things honest. I know there are times this is a tremendous challenge, but the benefit to the trust that is built has long-term effects. It is possible for us to violate this security, and then to rebuild it. But it is a long process.

The second essential element of a healthy marriage is found in Philippians 2:3-4 where Paul writes, *"Do nothing out of selfish ambition or vain conceit, but in humility consider others better than yourselves. Each of you should look not only to your own interests, but also to the interests of others."* The principle Paul addresses is meaningful communication

For some of us, it is easier for us to practice our faith and religion on a total stranger than it is to practice at home. Meaningful communication is essential to a marriage and a home. Meaningful communication is not simply a matter of talking more. Many couples have spoken hundreds of thousands of words to each other, but their marriage is no healthier today than it was five years ago. Meaningful communication involves the verbal and non-verbal communication and the willingness to really listen.

Research tells us only about 5% of the information coming through a conversation is communicated by verbal content, 38% of communication takes place thru vocal cues - tone of voice and 55% of the communication is by facial expression. Did you hear that men? Only 5% of our conversation is communicated through what we say, 93% is communicated by how we say it and our facial expression. Here is an area where our wives can really help us. This is also an area where we can do some real damage to a relationship. When it comes to meaningful communication, many men are intimidated by their wives. We know we are out of our league. Without knowing it ladies you have the ability to take all the wind out of our sails.

This usually happens whenever a husband tries to have meaningful communication with his wife and her face shows her disappointment of his effort. Wives you want to know a secret, something that will really spur your husband on? Sometime next week as he's driving home, these words will come to his mind. It normally takes about a week for us guys to figure things out. So he's in his car and it dawns on him, "So that's what that pastor meant?" And when he gets home he starts trying to have meaningful conversation with you. He's fumbling around making a fool out of himself, trying to find the right words. While he's trying, right in the middle of his attempt to open up, turn to him and say, *"Thanks hon. Boy I must be the luckiest woman in the world to be married to a guy like you."* Give him a kiss on the cheek and walk away. Then he'll run out to the garage and go, "Yeah, I did it! I've got this communication thing down pat! . . . . Now what was it I just did?"

You see gals, we guys want to have meaningful communication, we want to talk about the stresses and the problems, we want to honor you, but we're playing on a different ball field. It doesn't come naturally to us, but it is something we can <u>learn</u>. This is where security in your marriage comes into play. I've seen grown men who can take on the biggest baddest guys on the block, but they're afraid to talk to their wife. No one can have the influence on a man like his wife. And with just a little positive reinforcement of even the smallest of efforts, will give him the green light to keep trying. But meaningful communication takes time. So start slow and let it grow.

The Apostle Paul gives us another key ingredient to a healthy marriage in I Corinthians 7:3 where we read, *"The husband should fulfill his marital duty to his wife, and likewise the wife to her husband. The wife's body does not belong to her alone but also to her husband. In the same way, the husband's body does not belong to him alone but also to his wife. Do not deprive each other except by mutual consent and for a time, so that you may devote yourselves to prayer. Then come together again so that Satan will not tempt you because of your lack of self-control."* Here Paul addresses the principle of meaningful sexual and non-sexual touch.

There are times when a husband & wife will participate in the intimacies of marriage. And there are times when they should not. There are times when our touch ought to be non-sexual and just as meaningful. There have been a lot of books written on the differences between men and women in this area. One author talks about how men are like microwaves in their response to sexual intimacy and women tend to be more like crock-pots. It takes her much longer to warm up to the idea of sharing physical intimacies with her husband. Here's an area men, where our wives really need for us to understand them.

I have talked with many couples who have failed to understand the need for sexual and non-sexual touch. Husbands who are not mindful of the greater needs of their wife than just a romantic evening and wives who use sexual intimacy as a reward/punishment system. The healthy relationship will look for opportunities to practice small acts of touching. Holding hands on the way to the store, giving your husband or wife a hug & kiss before you leave for work. We will talk about sexual intimacy later in this book, but one of the areas we need to address here is the need to honor one another. In I Peter 3:7 we read, *"Husbands, in the same way be considerate as you live with your wives, and treat them with respect as the weaker partner and as heirs with you of the gracious gift of life, so that nothing will hinder your prayers."* When there is a healthy respect of our partner, many of the problems we will face can be easily resolved. Over the years I have been in too many homes, where the exterior looks grand, but inside there's emptiness. Oh, they still live together but its hell on earth for both of them. And when I retrace the steps that brought them to this point in their marriage, it often goes back to those early days when they just never got around to building honor and respect for one another.

God made a husband and wife different in so many ways in order for each to compliment the marriage. To bring something to the relationship the other could not provide. If both were identical, one of them is not necessary. And in today's culture, instead of enjoying the differences, we try our best to make everybody the same. And it doesn't work.

At the end of this chapter there is a worksheet of "Questions For Building A Healthy Marriage". It's far from extensive, but it may open the door to some dialogue that will bring benefit to your marriage. Look back to that verse out of Philippians, *"Each of you should look not only to your own interests but also to the interests of others."* We live in a world that conditions us to get what WE want out of every relationship. It's a sure fire receipt for disaster. To make our wedding day all we had hoped, we really need to start at the end. Focus on the real objective of the day, to begin building a life together as husband and wife.

Worksheet:
Building A Healthy Marriage

1. Do we spend enough time together?

2. What can we do to make better use of our time?

3. What do you consider meaningful communication?

4. How could I help improve our communication?

5. What have I done in the past that may have ruined meaningful communication?

6. How am I doing on my non-verbal communication?

7. How could I turn our arguments into something more constructive?

8. What is there about our relationship where I could help us to grow?

9. What are some ways I could understand what you are going through when you are hurting?

10. How could I help improve our decision making process?

Chapter Two

Bringing Our Past With Us

Each of us brings a past into our marriage. This may be a healthy past, often it is not. Try as we may to separate ourselves from the dysfunction of our family, or the hurts of our past, it is an issue we must deal with if our marriage will have any hope of being healthy and well balanced. The reality is we tend to carry some deep wounds within ourselves because of our past. Sometimes it's family issues, at other times it's just the pain of wrongs we suffered. Allow me to share a few issues couples have shared with me from their past: "My Dad told me he never wanted to see me again."

"I had an abortion when I was nineteen."

"My Mom left us when I was eleven."

"My uncle molested me when I was nine years old."

The events of our past can leave some deep scars in our psyche. Our wounds are often so deep we may not even know the influence they are having on us. And worse yet, we often repeat the very things that wounded us because we don't address the pain and seek to find a remedy that will bring healing to us and our future family. These wounds consist of hurtful memories, parental rejection or abandonment, a trusted family member who betrayed us or used us. Although it may be painful, opening up to the scars we carry before we tie the knot can be a healthy and even healing process.

The Bible tells us in I Peter 4:7, *"Therefore, be clear minded and self-controlled so that you can pray. Above all, love each other deeply, because love covers over a multitude of sin."* In other words, if we say we love one another and care for one another, we can be open about the wounds we are bringing into the relationship and help one another in the healing process. We often mistakenly think we need to keep our wounds a secret, that our future husband or wife doesn't need to know about what we have struggled with. But this is a mistake. Because if we're ever going to express deep love and commitment to one another, it begins by dealing with the influences of our past on our future relationships.

So where do we begin if we're going to heal the wounds of our past, if we're going to limit the dysfunction that has been in our life from influencing our future family? We begin by first identifying the events that have brought us pain, or the events that are influencing us today. Depending on how serious these wounds are, it is sometimes advisable to seek professional counseling. But the best place to begin is by talking about our past, the key events in our life and the memories that have influenced us. These events are not always bad. There are some memories we carry with us that have a tremendous influence in a positive way in our life. There are, for some of us, some deeply painful memories. It really does help to bring these out in the open. To let the light of truth begin to diminish their hold over us.

Just a word of caution: Every family has some measure of dysfunction. Because we are all just humans and we make mistakes. There is no perfect parent, no idealistic family, so be careful not to be too tough on the family. But there are also things that have happened in a family that need to be brought to the surface. And once we bring the events to the surface, we need to act on them. We need to take an action that will help build a healthy marriage and family.

Once we have identified our wounds, we need to forgive those who have offended us. Yes, I know this is a big request, but God has a plan for us. In I Peter 4:1 we read, *"Therefore, since Christ suffered in his body, arm yourselves also with the same attitude, because he who has suffered in his body is done with sin."* Notice the phrase, "the same attitude". God definitely understands the feelings we have when we have been hurt. This same passage tells us that Jesus *suffered*. There were the wounds that were visible but there were also the wounds that were not. The suffering He endured brought on by the betrayal of those who say they loved God, but called for His crucifixion. The one who looked Him in the face and said he would follow him anywhere and yet went and sold Him for thirty pieces of silver. The widen wounds we carry often take longer to heal than the visible.

God says when we get hurt, we need to hang onto the same attitude that Jesus had, the same way of thinking He had. So what were His thoughts? We can tell a lot about a person when they are under pressure. For most of us, when we're under pressure our true character, who we really are, what we really think shows. It was while Jesus was hanging on the cross he looked down at the very ones who had nailed Him to that cross and prayed, *"Father forgive them for they do not know what they're doing."* Make no mistake, He could have stopped the whole show. With a simple command, angels would have appeared to stop His suffering and punish those who were torturing Him. Instead He remained on the cross asking God to forgive His abusers. We forgive those who have offended us if we're ever going to be healed of our pain.

Now you may be saying, "I have no intention of forgiving those who've hurt me. They don't deserve it." And you would be right. Forgiveness is never deserved. But there are reasons why God wants us to try. The first being that He has forgiven us. All the times we have neglected Him, even abused our relationship with Him. And in exchange He offers us forgiveness. Not retaliation. As He has forgiven us, He wants us to do the same for others. If you're familiar with the Lord's prayer, part of that prayer says *"Forgive us our sins as we forgive those who've sinned against us."* Basically we are saying "Lord, forgive me in the same manner as I've forgiven everybody else."

The second reason for forgiving those who have hurt us is we're never going to stop our pain until we forgive. It's really the only way we can get rid of the hurt. For our own sake, not for theirs, we need to forgive. Hebrews 12:15 tells us, *"See to it that no one misses the grace of God and that no bitter root grows up to cause trouble and defile many."* Bitterness always hurts us more than it does the other person. We may hold onto a resentment over something that happened years ago. Meanwhile the offender has totally forgotten it. Resentment never hurts the other person, it hurts us. Job said, *"You're only hurting yourself with your anger."* And by holding onto that resentment, the power of that hurt still has control over us. Part of the reason God wants us to forgive is so we can move on with our own lives.

So to move on with life means we need a different focal point. In I Peter 4:2 we read, *"From now on, live the rest of your lives controlled by God's will, not by human desires."* God wants us to get our attention off ourselves, off our past, off of our pain and get the attention on to Him. Note the phrase, *"from now on"*, regardless of what has happened to us, regardless of the pain in our past, from now on focus on God's will. This calls for a major mental shift. When we've been hurt, we talk about us, about our pain, about how we feel. And if the truth be told, we often do not want to let go of the pain from our past because it gives us the leverage we need to keep all the attention on ourselves.

As a pastor I have had the opportunity to meet a lot of people who have had painful pasts. I have noticed a marked difference between those who are able to move on, and those who choose to live in the past. It's a choice of being a victim. Some of the people I have counseled have had horrendous things happen to them and yet they refuse to remain a victim. By doing so, they took the power away from the people who caused the pain and became empowered to move on with their lives. Others have had much less tragedy in their life, but seem to forever remain the victim. And by doing so they continue to empower the very people they despise for hurting them. It boils down to the choices we make.

Now you may be thinking, "So I'm just supposed to ignore my past?" And the answer is, of course not, there's no way we can do that. There's nothing wrong in feeling sadness over things that have happened to us. I am convinced this what Jesus had in mind when He said, *"Blessed are those who mourn for they shall be comforted."* There's a value in mourning, it shows sadness about the past and it is also a means by which we can release the past. We often get stuck in our pain because we focus on the hurt and not the Healer. God has the ability to bring a positive purpose out of our pain. Remember the story of Joseph and the coat of many colors?

His father had shown favor toward him and his brothers were jealous.So they did what any well respecting offended brothers would do, they sold Joseph into slavery. Joseph was taken to Egypt were he became a servant to Potipher, a very influential man. But Potiphers' wife made false accusations against Joseph that put him in prison, for two years. Eventually he was released, Pharaoh the ruler of Egypt, saw how good a leader he was, so he put Joseph in charge of running the country, including the distribution of food during a famine. Guess who shows up in the bread line? Joseph's brothers, the very ones who sold him into slavery. And though Joseph had the power and the opportunity to settle the score, he does just the opposite. When his brothers finally discover who he is, Joseph tells them, *"What you meant for harm, God meant for good."* Joseph was able to forgive his brothers, not because of anything they did to deserve his forgiveness, but because he kept his focus on God.

We often convince ourselves that God doesn't know about the things we have gone through. That somehow He is attentive to others, but not to us. Or maybe others deserve His attention, but we don't. But nothing could be further from the truth. In Psalm 56:8 we read, *"Record my lament; list my tears on your scroll— are they not in your record?"* The Bible tells us that God keeps a record of every tear we've ever cried. He's even kept track of the tears we couldn't cry because our pain or grief was so overwhelming. Our pain matters to God and He will settle the score the Bible tells us.

So what can we expect if we give our hurts and the wrongs people have done to us over to God? Romans 15:13 tells us, *"May the God of hope fill you with all joy and peace as you trust in Him so that you may overflow with the hope by the power of the Holy Spirit."* There are some great benefits to giving God our past. The first would be that our future marriage will not have this weight pressing down, putting unbelievable pressure on the marriage.

There are enough pressures a newly wed couple faces without allowing other forces to come into the relationship. Events and hurts that our mate had nothing to do with and is usually not even aware have happened. When we give our past to God, it sets us free to live life. To build a relationship that is not limited by the events that harmed us.

Some terrible things happened to Job in the Old Testament. He lost his children, his livelihood, even his health. And even his wife and friends turned against him. Job could have carried a lot of pain within himself, but in Job 11:13-16 we read, *"Put your heart right, reach out to God, then face the world again, firm and courageous. Then all your troubles will fade from your memory, like floods that are past and remembered no more."* Job knew that if he was ever going to be able to enjoy the now, he had to give God his past. And in fact Job was given more children, his livelihood was restored to him and the book ends by saying, *"And so Job died, old and full of years."* The key part to the verse is "full of years." It's only as we give God our past we can live a life *full of years*.

So after giving our past to God we're ready to change our future. To keep our present and future relationships from repeating the mistakes of the past we need some serious help. The first step is to put into action what the Bible tells us to do. In James 1:5 we read, *"If any of you lacks wisdom, he should ask God, who gives generously to all without finding fault, and it will be given to him."* Our first step toward a healthy marriage is to seek wisdom from God. This comes in a variety of ways.

One of the sources God provides to help us gain wisdom is the scriptures, the Bible. Yes, we often view the Bible as that heavy book we carried to Sunday School when we were kids. But now that we're adults we've outgrown its use. Besides the Bible is just a bunch of stuff about God, it doesn't really deal with real life. Well, reality is a little different than that.

Between the covers of this incredible book written over 4000 years, by forty different authors, is an abundance of insight dealing with a long list of real life issues. The real life record of people who had struggles quite similar to our own. The key to gaining wisdom is to look for the principles in each of the accounts. There's a reason why God led people to write the specific words and record the specific events they recorded. As we look for the principles in each event, what God did, what God expected, we gain insight to our own struggles as well.

Even this book is based on the principles I share with couples as I counsel them about the issues they face. Know in advance that it takes a while to accumulate this wisdom. I've been studying the scriptures for almost fifty years, and every time I dig into some issue, I find something I never saw before. The Bible is a storehouse of wisdom God wants us to tap into.

God has also provided godly teachers and counselors to help give us some direction. If we're serious about addressing specific issues our relationship faces, there are a wide variety of godly men and women who have written on the issues we are facing. It pays to hear what others have learned.

When my wife and I were first married (just after dirt was invented) I realized I had a lot of baggage from my family that would be very destructive to our relationship. I remember going to a couple's conference held at a little Baptist church in the town where we lived. It was like a Divine appointment, the two speakers talked about the very things I struggled with. And their insight opened the door for me to face and to change the family patterns from my past. I would like to say that I've got it all down pat, but that's far from the truth. I am, however, a lot further along because of what those godly teachers shared in that conference.

God uses His word, godly teachers, pastors and people, but there's one other source for God's wisdom. Our mate is a great source of wisdom. As we talk openly about the issues our relationship faces, God can use our mate to help direct our thinking. I know that it's a popular thing to joke about how little men understand women, or how little women understand men. But that diminishes the value of our differences. No one knows me better than my wife. We have been through the "thick and thin" of it all and she has earned the right for me to listen to her. It's really not uncommon that she will give me an insight about something that I missed. She sees things differently than I do and that difference compliments our marriage. And God uses that difference to bless both of us.

As we saw earlier, there may be issues that are bigger than we can handle on our own. If we're going to address these bigger issues we need to set some healthy boundaries. And one of the ways that we set healthy boundaries is getting support from people who have faced what we have faced. Proverbs 15:22 tells us *"Plans fail for lack of counsel, but with many advisers they succeed."* There are a wide variety of support groups that gather people who have gone through similar struggles, in order that we can encourage and equip one another to deal with the issues of our past. God never meant for any of us to solve our hurts on our own. Someone once said, "We're never fully healed until we're able to share our hurts with a fellow-struggler." As we grow, we can help others grow who need our help in their journey to deal with their past. Ecclesiastes 4:9 tells us, *"Two are better than one, because they have a good return for their work: If one falls down, his friend can help him up. But pity the man who falls and has no one to help him up!"* As we help each other through the journey of dealing with our past we not only find strength for ourselves, we give strength to others.

Many of us have wounds from our past. As we deal with these wounds it enables us to take our present relationships and our future relationships in an entirely different direction. The healing may take some time, but the benefits can be passed on to many generations.

Worksheet
Brining Our Past With Us

1. What kind of family setting did we have when we were growing up?

2. How are some of the most influential people is our lives?

3. What were their influences on us? The good and the bad?

4. How are the people in our family that have had the strongest influence on our overall family?

5. What is our family culture? What is our family's background?

6. What partners in relationships did we see demonstrated as we were growing up?

7. Are there issues we have faced in our past that will have an influence on our relationship?

8. What are the family patterns we would like to pass on to the next generation?

9. Do we both have trusted people we can confide in?

10. Is there any area of our relationship we want to be aware of in the future?

Chapter Three

A Touchy Subject

One of the toughest issues that newly weds face is managing their financial resources. In a survey conducted by George Gallup the survey revealed that the number one cause of arguments amongst couples is money. Sixty-five percent of all married couples argue about money. In fact, studies suggest that it is the leading cause of divorce. In a survey of people going through divorce, fifty-six percent said that their divorce was due in large part to money issues. This is a tough issue to tackle, but it is a battle worth fighting.

The issue of handling our finances is so significant; it would serve us well to have some wise counsel. Someone who knew how to handle money rightly, someone named Solomon. We know him as the wisest man who ever lived but he was also the wealthiest. On one occasion the Queen of Sheba brought him an honorarium of gold that was so large; it had to be brought to him on a barge. Solomon wrote a couple of books of counsel, one was the book of Ecclesiastes the other was the book of Proverbs. In these two books Solomon gives us some insight on how to stay out of trouble with our money.

In Proverbs 27:20, Solomon tells us why we get into financial trouble, *"Death and Destruction are never satisfied, and neither are the eyes of man."* His point is that one of biggest problems with finances is our insatiable hunger for more. Someone once asked Howard Hughes, "How much does it take to make a man happy?" To which he replied, "Just a little bit more." When you think about why we are always wanting more, it isn't the money itself; it's what we believe the money will bring us. We convince ourselves that money will bring three things:

First of all, we convince ourselves that having more money will bring us more happiness. If we look around, the advertising industry reminds us on a daily basis that if we have more, we're going to be happier. Solomon counsels us in Ecclesiastes 5:10, *"Whoever loves money never has money enough; whoever loves wealth is never satisfied with his income."* This constant desire to acquire, if left unchecked, will not only not bring us happiness, it can bring us ruin.

Secondly, we convince ourselves that money will bring us more respect or admiration or even fame. With enough money we can buy all the status symbols to let other people know how successful we are in life. But Jesus taught us in Matthew 16:26, *"What good will it be for a man if he gains the whole world, yet forfeits his soul? Or what can a man give in exchange for his soul?"* Someone once said we should never confuse our value with our valuables. With many of the rich & famous we see in the media, we often overlook the other areas of their life that have gotten out of control in order for them to maintain the image of "having it all."

Thirdly, we convince ourselves that more money will bring us more security. But we have seen in this country time after time, the fall of the stock market, the fall of real estate, and the fall of the net worth of millions who had convinced themselves that their money was their security. The reality is that we will never have the control over the financial industry to insure that our investments and our wealth is safe. And with that inability comes insecurity. Just recently one of the leading financial institutions in the U.S. announced it is considering laying off 45,000 employees because of a down turn in the real estate market. In light of that, look at what Solomon has to say in Proverbs 23:5 *"Cast but a glance at riches, and they are gone, for they will surely sprout wings and fly off to the sky like an eagle."* Solomon understood that money alone could not be trusted to bring security, because we can't control all the forces that bring us the money or take the money from us. Thus we cannot count on our finances to be a source of security. Solomon goes on to give us counsel in other areas of our finances.

In Ecclesiastes 5:11 Solomon counsels us, *"As goods increase, so do those who consume them. And what benefit are they to the owner except to feast his eyes on them?"* Another translation reads, *"The richer you are the more mouths you have to feed."* The reality is that the more we have, the more it takes to keep what we have. The insurance, the taxes, the accountants, and the attorneys all cost. The cost of wealth increases in proportion to the wealth. Howard Hughes spent millions every year to "protect" the millions that he had. And that's not taking into consideration the emotional price tag of protecting his wealth.

Solomon goes on in Ecclesiastes 5:12, *"The sleep of a laborer is sweet, whether he eats little or much, but the abundance of a rich man permits him no sleep."* Along with the greater abundance comes greater worry. When the market goes down, we worry about how much we're losing. When oil prices go up, we worry about how much it costs to drive the "mansion on wheels" to grandma's house. How much will it cost us this year to insure it, to pay the taxes on it, to pay the accountant for keeping track of all of it?

Notice how Solomon compares the sleep of a laborer to the lack of sleep of the rich man. The guy or gal working nine-to-five goes to work, punches the time clock, puts in their day, their shift ends, they go home and have a great nights sleep. Meanwhile, the business owner goes home and worries. In fact they probably went to the office early just to get a jump on the demands for the day. Then they stay late to finish up another report. Then on the way home they run through all the details of the day and worry that the state was satisfied, the Feds were satisfied, that Workers Comp was satisfied, and oh yeah, did we turn a profit today?

Solomon is not trying to discourage any of us from working hard and providing for our families. He is addressing the dream that we often have, that if we just had more, we'd be better off. Solomon goes on in Ecclesiastes 5:14 and says, *"I have seen a grievous evil under the sun: wealth hoarded to the harm of its owner, or wealth lost through some misfortune, so that when he has a son there is nothing left for him."* Solomon's warning is that if we are counting on our money and things to bring us significance and security, we are going to be greatly disappointed.

Solomon would be among the first to counsel us to provide for our families, he goes on to counsel us on how to be good managers of our money, regardless of how much we make. In Proverbs 27:23 Solomon says, *"Be sure you know the condition of your flocks, give careful attention to your herds; for riches do not endure forever, and a crown is not secure for all generations."* I particularly like that phrase, *"know the condition of your flock"*. In other words, Solomon wants us to keep track of our money, and to know the condition of our finances.

Many couples start their marriage in a fog. Convinced that love will carry them through. Granted, love must be the foundation upon which any couple will build a marriage and a family. But the old saying holds true, "Love doesn't pay the rent!" Knowing our financial condition is critical to the success of a marriage. If I hear someone say, "I just don't know where all my money goes." That is a sure sign that something is wrong with the financial managing skills in that family.

One of the conversations every couple should have before tying the knot is not only about how much money is going to be coming in, but how much is going out and how will the family financial records be kept. Most of the counseling I have done with newly weds about their finances, normally boils down to someone not knowing all the details and the one who has been left in the dark is offended.

So one of the first things to do as you talk about finances is to find out what each of you owe, what each of you will earn, how much are the payments and how will you *"know the condition of your flock'.* It doesn't hurt to get in the habit of writing down on a Family Finances Book, all the numbers. Even when they don't seem to matter.

When my wife and I were first married, a friend who happened to be a banker gave us some great advice. It was during a time when we didn't have much money coming in and things were kind of tight. His counsel was, "Write down everything you spend money on. If you buy a pack of gum, it goes on the pad." We've found that's a good plan regardless of how little or how much we are making. We have to know the details of our financial condition.

Solomon goes on to say in Proverbs 21:5, *"The plans of the diligent lead to profit as surely as haste leads to poverty."* His point being that we must plan our finances. Financial planning is not normally a part of our wedding day plans. There is a marked difference between couples who are less stressed about finances than those who are highly stressed about finances; it normally boils down to planning. Planning the income and planning the outgo. Nothing will get any of us in trouble faster than not planning our buying, especially when it's big purchases. An interesting survey in 2004, showed that women made more purchases, but men made bigger purchases. And to make any purchases of any size without knowing the "condition of our flocks" sets the stage for financial disaster. But note what else Solomon says in that passage, *"haste leads to poverty"*. Advertising people call that "impulse buying". It is their number one objective in advertising, to entice us to see it on the screen or on a billboard and rush to the store to buy it now! And buying on impulse is like eating on impulse; both will leave you fat, unhappy and broke. This is where open communication is so important to your long term success. Maybe one of you knows that you are an impulsive shopper. Now is the time to talk about that with your future spouse! Yes, it may be a little uncomfortable, but being open now, may save you a lot of tears later on.

At the end of this chapter is a simple Financial Game Plan. It's intended to be a sample, a starting point for planning your finances. You may have something better. The point is start now making a plan for your finances and the benefits will be enormous. But Solomon goes on to give us just a few more pieces of advice on finances.

In Proverbs 13:11 Solomon says, *"Dishonest money dwindles away, but he who gathers money <u>little by little</u> makes it grow."* This is a principle we Americans really have a tough time with, the principle of saving. Whereas families in Europe save around 16% of their annual income, we Americans save less than 5% of our annual income. This sets the stage for real disasters to happen in the life of a family. Without a savings to fall back on, whenever there is an emergency, i.e. the transmission goes out in the family car, the frig stops refrigerating, or any other host of unforeseen crisis, we Americans resort to the number one financial killer – credit cards! Untold millions (even billions) in finance charges and interest accumulated could be kept in our family budget if we

Americans could only avoid our dependency on credit cards. By simply setting aside even a small amount on a regular basis, we could save ourselves millions of dollars in comparison to the 20, 25 or even 30% in interest charged by credit card companies.

Just recently Congress brought in the heads of the largest credit card companies in America and deplored their abuse of the American public. With harsh words and ominous threats the men and women of Congress put the pressure on these business leaders to lower their excessive fees and exuberant interest rates. Promises were made, the hearings concluded and the credit card companies went right back to what they had been doing. Because we Americans will pay the incredible interest rates, late fees and hidden charges.

If it sounds as if I have a problem with the credit card industry, you are right. Dozens of couples I have counseled have gotten themselves in trouble <u>day one</u> of their marriage because they relied on credit cards instead of listening to Solomon and start working on setting aside *"little by little"*. Someone once said, "The secret to financial freedom is not how much you make, its how much you keep." If we're using credit cards, we're keeping less as the credit card companies make more.

In Proverbs 21:25 Solomon counsels us, *"The sluggard's craving will be the death of him, because his hands refuse to work. All day long he craves for more, but the righteous give without sparing."* The principle Solomon is addressing is contentment. Whereas the sluggard is constantly needing more to be "happy" Solomon shows us that the wise financial manager is different. They enjoy their work, their livelihood because they know the value of enjoying what they have without "craving" for something else to be happy.

Again this is a tough issue for us Americans. We stretch ourselves too thin, buying things we don't really need, with money we don't really have, in order to make payments that we can't really afford. Have you ever notice how easy it is to get into debt and how difficult to get out? Note Solomon's words, *"The sluggard's craving will be the death of him ...."* Learning to enjoy what we have takes the pressure off of constantly needing to buy the latest "thing" in order to be happy.

Our fixation in America of having the latest & greatest has put our entire nation into financial trouble. And it may sound strange that the wealthiest man who ever lived should counsel us in Ecclesiastes 3:13, *"That everyone may eat and drink, and find satisfaction in all his toil—this is the gift of God."* That counsel goes contrary to what we practice in this country. Working and providing for our families is seen more as a drudge than a joy. But there is a secret to enjoying our labor, enjoying the little that we have. And that secret is this: Each time we build on what we already have, it is sweeter than having it all right now.

As I was growing up, I watched by grandfather go to work six days a week, put in a full days work and then come home at night dog tired. He did that for 40 years. Then when he retired, when he had more than enough money to sit back and relax, he called up the company where he had worked and asked if he could come back to work on a part-time basis. He found satisfaction in his work and enjoyment in the friends he worked with. He was sixty-eight years old before he ever bought a "new" car. He modeled the value of *"finding satisfaction in all his toil..."* and not depending on another "thing" to bring him satisfaction. Solomon gives us one more piece of financial counsel.

36

In Proverbs 3:9 Solomon says, *"Honor the Lord with your wealth, with the firstfruits of all your crops; then your barns will be filled to overflowing, and your vats will brim over with new wine."* Now you may be saying, "I knew it, this is a typical pastor wanting us to give our money to the church." Well, that's not quite the case. Solomon's counsel is all about priorities. Where our money goes is a good indicator of our priorities.

Why would Solomon ever give this kind of counsel on finances, especially when just starting out a couple doesn't normally have a lot of discretionary money? Well, the simple answer to that is that Solomon knew the source of his wealth. He was well aware that God was his provider. And without God's blessing his wealth could disappear over night.

If for no other reason, giving back to God a portion of what we have earned is an act of gratitude. It demonstrates the priority of putting the things of God first in our family. In Matthew 6:31 Jesus teaches us, *"So do not worry, saying, 'What shall we eat?' or 'What shall we drink?' or 'What shall we wear?' For the pagans run after all these things, and your heavenly Father knows that you need them. But seek first his kingdom and his righteousness, and all these things will be given to you as well."* Notice His words, "all these things will be given to you". God is mindful of our needs. He wants us to see the reality that He is our Provider. Yes, He has given us the ability to think, some of us have talent in different industries, but the bottom line always comes back to God. Without His provision in our life, we would not have the intellectual, emotional, gifting ability to do anything in this life.

Notice that Solomon counsels us to *"give of the firstfruits of all your crops",* in other words don't give the leftovers to God. He deserves to be first place in our life and we demonstrate that by the use of our finances. And before you say, "I can't afford to give to God." Solomon's answer would be, "You can't afford not to." If we want God to bless our laborers, if we want to escape the worry of what shall we eat or what shall we wear, then we must have God's blessing. And if we want God to bless, we put Him first in our finances.

With all the counsel that Solomon has given us, we may overlook the value of his counsel. In Proverbs 19:8 we read, *"He who gets wisdom loves his own soul; he who cherishes understanding prospers."* If the battle for peace in our finances is going to be won, it's as we listen to those who have the wisdom to give us an "edge" in winning. And of all the people who have ever lived that have earned the right to be heard, Solomon fits that bill. The word "cherish" means to hold close to, to count as valued. As we hold close Solomon's insight to money, we will prosper. That may not mean incredible wealth that may mean peace in our marriage – which is worth much.

Worksheet:
Our Financial Game Plan

Income

His . . . .   _____

Hers . . . .   _____

2nd Jobs . . . .   _____

Additional . . . . .   _____

Total A . . . .   _____

Outgo

Gods Use . . . . . .   _____

Housing . . . .   _____

Savings . . . .   _____

Car Payments . .   _____

Utilities . . . .   _____

Food . . . .   _____

Insurance . . . . .   _____

Other Bills . . . .   _____

Total B . . . .   _____

Total C . . . .   _____
Subtract Total B
from Total A =
Discretionary Cash

Worksheet:
Our Long Term
Financial Game Plan

Total C . . . .   _____

Presently

      Savings . . . .   _____

      401K . . . .   _____

      Stocks/Bonds . . . . .   _____

      Other . . . .   _____

                  Total D . . . . _____

Equity

      Home . . . .   _____

      Other Real Estate . .   _____

      Vehicles . . . .   _____

      Other . . . .   _____

                  Total E . . . . _____

                  Net worth . . . . _____
                  Total C, D, E

Chapter Four

Have A Great Sex Life

In my office I keep a candy dish. It was the candy dish my great grandmother would use to play a game with me. The game was, when I came to visit, she would hide the candy dish. My job was to go find it. After finding the dish, I would take it to my grandmother, she would tease me and we would laugh together, then she would give me a piece of candy from the dish. The question I ask couples is this, "What are the memories I have attached to this candy dish? Getting the candy or laughing and being with my great-grandmother?" And most often couples will choose, "laughing and being with your grandmother." And they are absolutely right. I use the dish to help couples see the difference between good sex and a great sex life. In many ways the candy dish represents the physical relationship between a husband and wife. Sometimes we are satisfied only to go and get candy out of the dish. When in fact there is so much more we could have.

There's a school of thought that has been around for quite sometime, it teaches that the sexual relationship in marriage was something that became a part of marriage because of sin. Therefore since sex originated in sin, couples should participate in sexual activities only for the express purpose of procreation, and for no other reason. I didn't attend that school. In fact, to get a thorough understanding of sex in marriage we need to go back to where it originated. Let's go back to the Garden of Eden, the first couple to ever file for a marriage license. In Genesis 1:28 we read, *"So God created man in his own image, in the image of God he created him; male and female he created them. God blessed them and said to them, "Be fruitful and increase in number; fill the earth and subdue it."* Notice, these instructions were given *before* sin came into the picture.

In fact Genesis 1:31 goes on to tell us, *"God saw all that He made and it was very good."* Now this is different than God's response to making the fish, the birds, and the animals of the field. Genesis records that when God surveyed that part of creation His reaction was, *"It was good."* But when He made man and woman, when He gave instructions to be fruitful and multiply He viewed that as *"Very good"*. So God came up with the idea of sex in marriage. Long before sin ever raised its ugly head God intended for husbands and wives to enjoy the intimacies of marriage.

Jesus continued that same view of marriage in Matthew 19:5, *"For this reason a man shall leave his father and mother, be united with his wife and the two shall become one."* Jesus taught about the need of a man to leave his father & mother and cleave to his wife. And in that process the two become one flesh. The union of a husband and wife happens on many different levels; the emotional, the spiritual, the intellectual, and the physical. What God started in the Garden, has God's blessing and approval. Unfortunately we often foul-up something that was so pure and good.

The physical act of marriage is a valid sanctified part of marriage. Jesus goes on to add in that same teaching to say, *"What God joins together let no man separate."* God approves of the physical union between husband and wife. And this union is more than just sex; it is the act of marriage. Sex may best describe what happens between unwed people, but it does not come close to describing the fulfillment two people can enjoy when they share in the right way what God has designed.

Once we understand how God designed us to participate in the sexual act of marriage, we have the potential to express something in the act of marriage that is more than just a biological function. I am convinced that the act of marriage was designed by God to be one of the most satisfying fulfilling experiences two people can share together on this earth. And the thinking among some Christian circles that sexual activity is only for producing children and if we actually enjoy what we're doing means we have a perverted mind, is rubbish. What God has designed and blessed, we can enjoy! Now to enjoy all God intended we need to be reminded of a couple of things.

First of all we need to understand the human body. Let's remember that Adam & Eve were not given a manual on sexual behavior. You know what God did? He told them, "Learn By Doing". Now it's true they had 900 years to practice, we don't. In a time when so much attention is focused on the form and function of the sexual relationship, we lose track that all the parts were designed by God.

Many of the couples I counsel, when asked point blank, confide in me that they have participated in sexual activity prior to the wedding day. Amazingly, the number one justification is they want to make sure they are sexually compatible. To which my response is, "Trust me on this one, all the parts will fit. Our Designer made them to fit well together, you don't have to worry." There is something to be said for waiting until our sexual activity falls under the umbrella of God's intended design. Jesus was very clear on this when He said, "What God joins together . . ." meaning that under the blessing of being husband and wife, our sexual relationship finds its greatest fulfillment. No guilt, no regrets, no need to hide.

Now I know you didn't buy this book, or you are not reading this book in order to hear some pastor give you the "old fashion" sermon about waiting. But I have sat with too many young couples, when I ask the question, "Have you been sexually involved with one another?" And I watch their eyes tear up and their face show the signs of disappointment. Not my disappointment, but their own. There's something to be said about a bride and groom walking down the aisle, meeting in the presence of witnesses, standing before God and entering their marriage with a clean slate. Now before you say, "it's too late we've already crossed that threshold." God can restore what has been lost.

Here's what I suggest for couples who have been sexually active prior to their wedding day. Step one, stop! Sit down together and recommit yourselves to one another. Agree that your sexual relationship is best fulfilled under God's blessing. And agree that you will abstain from sexual activity until your wedding night. Step two, tell someone. I know this is tough, but our sexual impulse is incredible strong. And couples who have been sexually active, who know one another on a sexual level, have an even more difficult battle. By telling one other person, we're asking for accountability. We're asking for someone to help us keep a commitment we have made to our future marriage partner. Step three, guard yourselves. Start spending more time with people. Go on double dates, go out with a group of friends or sit in the living room at her parents' home. Do whatever you must do to guard yourselves sexually. The benefits from this effort will be extremely satisfying.

Allow me to illustrate. I met with Jim and Sandy (not their real names) for pre-marital counseling about six months prior to their wedding day. In our session together I asked what I always ask, "Have you been sexually involved with one another?" With disappointment in their voices they both shared how things just got out of control and they had been sexually active on several occasions. I asked if they would care to restore their relationship so that they could enjoy all of Gods blessing on their marriage, to which they both agreed. That evening they both committed themselves to abstaining from sexual activity until their wedding day.

Poor Jim must have called me a dozen times over the next few weeks. We talked about a lot of things, but most of our conversations were his attempt to keep his commitment to his future wife. The day of the wedding finally came, much to Jim's relief. As Sandy walked down the aisle, Jim was awe struck at how incredibly beautiful his bride looked. As we got into the vows, everything was going well until I ask Jim to repeat after me, *"I Jim . . . have you Sandy . . . to be my wedded wife . . . to have and to hold . . . "* I never heard the words "to have and to hold" when I looked up, Jim was sobbing. As he looked at his bride he told me later, he saw the woman he truly loved. And he realized that their wedding was more than a legal formality, it was their moment to stand before God and receive his blessing. He also realized how glad he was that they had recommitted themselves to waiting for their wedding day.

By the way, Jim is not the only groom to ever have a tough time keeping his emotions in check while saying his vows.

There is much for us to understand about our physical bodies and the sexual activity we will be involved with. There are a number of excellent Christian authors who have written on the subject of understanding the physical part of marriage. With all the pressure our culture puts on our sexual activity, it's amazing how ill informed we are about the male and female anatomy. I encourage newly weds locate some good reading material for better understanding the human body. The best time to learn is just before your marriage.

Secondly we need to understand the value of the act of marriage to the other person. Most husbands *think* they know what sexual intimacy means to their wife, and most wives *think* they know what it means to their husband. Let's look at a couple of things for a second:
The act of marriage is obviously going to help satisfy a man's

sex drive, which is strongest from age eighteen to twenty-five. There is a time when his sex drive is stronger than his wife's. But sexual activity in marriage also helps a man fulfill his manhood. That sounds real corny but be careful here. A man has a strong and yet highly impressionable ego. Wives you want him to have a strong ego. It nudges him to action. You'll find that if he does not find his satisfaction in the act of marriage it will be a threat to his ego. A good healthy relationship with his wife will also stimulate his love for his wife. The act of marriage also provides a man with life's most exciting and fulfilling experience.

For the wife sexual activity in marriage satisfy's needs as well. The act of marriage was not designed solely for masculine gratification. It was designed by God for mutual gratification. Wives will find that sexual activity in marriage helps fulfill her self image. She has a natural sex drive as well. Studies show that in many cases her sex drive increases about the age of thirty-five to thirty-seven, just about the time his is declining, often creating an interesting series of events. A wife's sex drive is affected by: a monthly cycle, estrogen levels and other factors. There are times a wife will initiate the encounter, which is perfectly normal and healthy. As well as meeting a natural desire, the act of marriage also reassures a wife of her husbands love. When the act of marriage is participated in the right manner it satisfies not only a physical need but an emotional need as well. As for the husband, the act of marriage provides the wife one of lives most exciting physical experience. Remember it is for mutual gratification.

One thing that relates to both husband and wife, the act of marriage provides an experience that is exclusively shared between the two. We share our partners in a lot of ways: their looks, their talents and abilities. Our friends and family, the people at the office all enjoy our mate's sense of humor, their willingness to care for others or a host of other character qualities, which make them who they are. Only the act of marriage is designed to be exclusively shared between a husband and wife. And by the way, the degree of satisfaction in the sexual relationship between a husband and wife has no relationship with world statistics. Sociologists have concluded that the average married couple participates in the act of marriage 4.3 times per month. (I'm not real sure about the .3 times.) But world statistics mean nothing to your relationship it is exclusive between the two of you.

With all that's been said on the sexual relationship, allow me to suggest a couple of things. First to husbands:

Husbands, practice self control. In most cases you will be initiating the sexual activity; you need to practice the control. Recognizing that your wife's responses are different than yours. Men for example are stimulated by what they see; women are stimulated by kind words and a gentle touch. I think it is significant that Jesus should say to a man, *"Not to lust after a woman."* Men are attracted by what they see. That's why a man and wife can have a little spat over dinner; he goes to the garage or living room, she goes to the family room. They work around the house for a while. Finally he heads to the bedroom, she comes in disrobes, combs her hair, turns off the light and gets in bed. He rolls over, puts his arm around her and he's ready for? A romantic evening! What's she ready for? Sleep! Men how do we solve that problem? Self Control.

Secondly men, seek your wife's satisfaction not just your own. In the early years of a marriage it is easy for a man to be satisfied biologically. But a man who loves his wife will not be emotionally satisfied until she is also satisfied in the act of marriage. In the early years of marriage it may take some time to help each other rid ourselves of inhibitions. A young man shared with me about how he and his wife seldom shared in the act of marriage. As I counseled with them, I discovered that this young bride had never seen her father hold or kiss or show any sign of affection to her mother. These are the kinds of issues this young husband and wife had to face together. It may take some time to get rid of some of the inhibitions. Regardless of what late night talk shows may say, a fulfilling sex life is a gradual learning process. Take the time to learn from your wife what is satisfying and fulfilling to her.

Finally guys, remember what stimulates a woman, kind words and a gentle touch. Charlie Shedd is one of my favorite authors. Charlie was well into his sixties when he wrote his book on Christian Marriage. He tells of the day he woke up and decided, that day, he was going to prepare his wife for a romantic evening. So he got up, came down to breakfast stopped his wife, gave her a long passionate kiss, said nothing to her, but instead went upstairs and took a shower. On his way out the front door he embraced his wife gave her a special kiss and then with that twinkle in his eye he said, "I'll be home early tonight." During the day he sent her flowers, bought her a gift and called her often. Charlie tells that evening they had one of the most romantic evenings they could imagine. Of course this is the same guy who came to bed on one occasion dressed as a pirate. Charlie is a great example that our sex life was intended to be enjoyed, not just biologically, but emotionally as well.

To the wives allow me to say, maintain a positive mental attitude. It's amazing the number of Christian woman who have been biased toward the sexual act of marriage by some well meaning aunt who led them to believe that their wedding night was something that simply had to be "endured". God never intended for wives to simply endure sexual involvement with their husbands, He intended for them to enjoy their husbands.

Allow yourself some time to adjust to your husband. And be patient as he learns as well. He may not know how to talk about sexual issues or he may be uncomfortable asking about what brings you satisfaction. Look for those occasions when you can bring to his attention something that you enjoy, or something that makes you feel uncomfortable. Remember God intended that act of marriage to be mutually satisfying.

Secondly, remember what stimulates a man. Your husband is more visually stimulated so it's not unusual for him to be interested in a romantic evening simply because you came to bed dressed in a flannel night gown. Your husband is much quicker to be ready for sexual activity, so don't think it strange or weird that he has the ability to turn "on" as quickly as he does. All of these are areas that he will need to learn from you, and you will need to learn about him. Remember what stimulates.

For both of you, learn to communicate freely. This may be uncomfortable in the early days of your marriage. But it's in the early days you can begin to build good communication, especially in your sexual activity. And open communication goes a long way in bringing a satisfying and fulfilling sexual relationship to both of you.

And this may sound a little strange, but when in doubt, pray. After all, the one who came up with the idea of sexual activity in marriage was God. He designed it, He intends for us to enjoy our marriage partner. In addition, God is concerned with every detail of your life. So to ask God to show us how to be a better husband, or a better wife, to show us how to be more loving and to help our mate find more satisfaction in our marriage, is not a stretch at all. One of my favorite authors, Tim LaHaye, tells of a young couple who had reached a snag in their physical relationship. They were unsure what to do, or how to solve the problem they were facing. Both agreed to pray about their problem. One evening they were invited to a get together at some friend's home. Arriving first they were escorted to the family room where they were seated behind a huge floral arrangement. A short time later another couple came in, thinking they were alone, sat down and starting talking about a problem they had, the identical problem the first couple was struggling with. The second couple went on to talk about the book they had read, what it had meant to them and how it changed them. Meanwhile the first couple was frantically looking for a pen to write down the name of that book. God wants us to enjoy the intimacies of marriage He designed for us.

Let's go back to the candy dish for just a minute. It's not just the candy in the dish that is worth having, it's the dish itself. The real satisfaction in the sexual activity in marriage is not the physical act alone, it's the intimacy. It's the closeness that only the two of you can share. Over the years the physical activity will change. In some seasons of your marriage you will be very sexually active, it other seasons your intimacy will take on a different form. But there's something to be said about looking across the pillow early in the morning and watching your wife, the woman you have spent thirty-five years of life with. Thirty-five years of learning and growing and even changing, and knowing that the two of you share something that is only between the two of you.

Worksheet
Developing Intimacy

1. How is our non-sexual relationship? Are we open to one another? Do we talk about even the uncomfortable things?

2. Are we waiting for our wedding day? How do both us of feel about this?

3. What are the influences on these areas of our relationship?

4. Do we feel "honored" by one another?

5. Do we spend enough "meaningful" time together?

6. What would be a Romantic evening for you?

7. What would you change about our physical relationship if you could?

8. What are some of our fondest memories of our time together?

9. Are we preparing ourselves for a meaningful sexual relationship?

10. Do we need to spend more time with others to insure our sexual conduct is appropriate?

Chapter Five

How To Have A Good Fight

Have you had your first fight yet? How did it work for you? Did you just drop the issue and let things cool down? Did you learn anything about yourself, about your future partner? Allow me to introduce you to this couple I know. Two people who love one another and, regardless what one may say, the other always agree. Conversations go like this, "Where do you want to go tonight?" "I don't care where do you want to go?" "It doesn't matter to me, as long as I'm with you." "Anywhere is fine with me, just so long as I'm with you." (I'm a little nauseous.) Before they're married there's never a cross word, but six months later, the *fur's a flyin'* and there's a constant battle going on in that home. Why the big change? Part of the reason is some of us grew up in a home where arguments never happened. There was just this pent up anger that lay boiling just beneath the surface. Some of us grew up in homes where the "fur flew" on a regular basis, and we see nothing wrong with letting it all out when the heat of marital battle begins. Reality is there will be tension and conflict in a marriage. Its two different people we're talking about here.

There will be a time when there will be a good ole' husband & wife heated discussion. Probably over something that didn't mean anything in the long run. The greatest danger about a fight is that no one would win. No, not win as we usually think, but I mean really win. Now make no mistake, some of us are content only if we win; if the other person accepts defeat, if we have the last word and if we have our way, then we win. But most of the time we don't stop to consider how our many victories are adding up to one gigantic defeat. There's many a Christian couple who have read Bible and applied it to church or their walk with God, but they never took it home. Someone once said, "If our religion doesn't work at home, it doesn't work, don't try to export it." The Bible has an abundance of insight on how to get the most out of life, not just when we die and go to heaven, but here and now. Even on how we can have good come out of our family fights.

Jesus taught about the danger of unresolved conflict in our home. In Mark 3:25 He we read, *"A home filled with strife and division destroys itself."* There's a real danger with conflict. Conflict can kill a marriage. We all know there's going to be conflict in a marriage. We know it's going to happen, we just don't think it's going to happen to us. The Bible has lot to say on understanding conflict and resolving them in a way that benefits our marriage and our lives.

The first has to do with why we have conflict, why we become angry with the people we love in the first place. The Bible says, it's all about ME. James 4:1 tells us, *"Do you know where your fights and arguments come from? They come from the selfish desires that war within you."* The Bible is very clear about this; it's almost blunt, as a matter of fact. It's our selfishness that is the root of the tension and the conflicts in all our relationships. We want, what we want, and we want it, now. And we won't be happy until it happens.

On our wedding day there were unspoken expectations. When we said, "I do", there were expectations that went along with those vows. Without even knowing it, we may be saying, "This is how this marriage is going to meet my needs." And somehow we convince ourselves into thinking that as soon as we get to know each other a little bit, things will work out. Then the longer we're married and the closer we get to each other, the more we begin to recognize the differences in the other person's life.

The more we stay focused on the differences, the more opportunity there is for conflict. This is just part of our human nature. We would like to think, if the other person would just do what we tell them, everybody would be happier. But we would be way off. Because there will be always something else, some other need we have, some other expectation we set that they must fulfill. And thus the root cause of anger, of arguments and unresolved conflict is still within us.

Now before you say, "Boy this is really encouraging. I can tell the married life is not for me." There is a solution to the problem. And the solution is not "giving in" all the time, which can also be very unhealthy. The truth is there are some things that are worth fighting for in our marriage, issues that are brought to the surface only when the pressure of conflict is applied. In fact, let me go on record here, we never really get everything out of our marriage until we have traversed the "mine field" of heated exchange, of arguments. So the question is not how do we avoid arguments, the greater question is, how can we get our arguments to work for us?

The Bible addresses this very issue. In Ephesians 4:25 the Apostle Paul gives us some guidelines on how to have a good fight. We might call them the "Seven Rules For a Good Fight". Even when countries go to war, there are "Rules Of War" things that countries have agreed are acceptable and things that are not. If we're going to make the most of the conflicts in our marriage, let's play by the rules.

In v. 25 Paul writes, *"Therefore, each of you must put off falsehood and speak truthfully . . . "* So the first principle he gives us, is to commit ourselves to honesty and respect. To get the most mileage out of heated exchange, we have to agree in advance that we will go into that exchange with an agenda. And the first item on that agenda is we will be honest with one another and we will respect one another. Without a doubt this is where many of the couples I have counseled have failed to begin. For whatever reasons, we often harbor a lack of respect for our marriage partner. And without respect, honesty is wasted. Without respect, honesty becomes a ball bat or a battering ram. Honesty becomes destructive. In Hebrews 13:4 we read, *"Have respect for marriage. Always be faithful to your partner. . ."* We may not have seen others demonstrate respect for their marriage partner, but that does not give us a license to do the same.

When I was a much younger pastor, I watched a man who was forever belittling his wife in the presence of others. His little jabs and put-downs may have entertained others, but I could see on his wife's face she had heard too much of it. When I said something to the husband, his defense was, "I'm just teasing her. She's knows I don't mean anything by it." But the reality was that he did mean something by it. And eventually his wife divorced him. Not because he didn't provide for her, not because she didn't have a nice house, but simply because her husband had no respect for her.

Honesty and respect are born out of a spirit of "This is my equal." In that same book of Ephesians, Paul tells us to "speak the truth in love." His implication is that we are on equal ground when we come to marital conflict. So when coming to the fight, get armed with truth, but be motivated by respect. And one of the biggest hurdles to marital conflict will already be overcome.

Paul goes on in Ephesians 4:26 to teach us, *"In your anger do not sin . . . . and do not give the devil a foothold."* This is a passage that New Testament scholars call a permissive imperative. Which means God is not commanding us to blow our top; He permits anger that does not lead to sin. Here Paul's counsel is that we would choose our weapons wisely. There are an assortment of weapons in our arsenal that can be used in the heat of an argument. Some of these weapons are deadly. We know how lethal they can be. We know they are weapons that can do immense damage to the other person. Yet we use them anyway. Those weapons would include:

> Anger expressed in profanity.
> Anger that attacks ones self worth.
> Anger that focuses on known weaknesses.
> Anger that reaches back to past mistakes.
> Using of "never" and "always" to describe feelings or actions. And that's just the short list.

Solomon was insightful when he wrote in Proverbs 18:14, 19, *"A man's spirit sustains sickness, but a crushed spirit who can bear?" An offended brother is more unyielding than a fortified city."* Have you ever had a wounded or crushed spirit? It hurts doesn't it? When we attack the person rather than the problem, when we resort to any and all weapons in the heat of an argument, we'll only crush the other person. And the end result is, we may win the skirmish, we may get our way, but we're setting the groundwork for a ruined marriage.

Notice where Paul says: *"Do not give the devil a foothold."* A foothold in your marriage? How do any of us ever allow the devil entrance to our marriage? There are least three footholds:

Living In Denial, "I don't have problem, they have the problem." "Our marriage is perfect. If everybody does I as say, everything will be fine, and we'll all be happier." There are many forms of denial. But living in denial leaves the door open for the Deceiver to get a better grip on your marriage.

Inappropriate Confiding, a survey taken several years ago revealed that 80% of all adulterous relationships began when friends "confided" in someone other than their marriage partner · about problems they were having in their marriage. To share your "story" with someone of the opposite sex is giving the devil a key to the door of your marriage.

Dredging Up The Past, continually using past mistakes as leverage in an argument serves as a constant reminder to your mate, "Things will never get better. You've blown it in the past and I'm keeping track of every mistake you make." Certainly the devils Number One goal is to convince us, "Why Try? Things will never get better. Quite while you're ahead." Avoiding dredging up the past really calls for a change in priorities. If the priority is to win, then keep the past alive. But if the priority is to grow from our conflict, to make our marriage better from our conflict, then let the past be the past. Nobody likes to be reminded of the mistakes they made yesterday. And the reality is, today we are all different people because of what we have learned from our mistakes.

Paul goes on in Ephesians 4:26 to tell us, *"Do not let the sun go down while you are still angry. . ."* The principle he gives us in choose the right time for our fights. There's a good time for an all out battle of the will and there's a not so good time. Paul has in mind timeliness, rather than a particular time of the day. Notice this follows his instruction about respect and honesty. Two people who want a disagreement or argument to be productive, to accomplish something other than two people *fighting to the death*, will understand the need to pick a good time. "After the kids have gone to bed" "After we take a walk around the block" "After we adjust from a hectic day" Our mate will send up the "battle flag" if we're watching. It comes in a variety of ways; some of us get quiet, hoping we'll be asked about our silence. For some of us, minor irritations bring out an extreme reaction, a sure sign there's something that needs to be addressed. Whatever signals we may use, choosing the right time to have a heated discussion goes a long way to reveal the real purpose for the exchange.

If we're just interested in "blowing off steam" and we don't really want the conflict to help us grow as a couple, any place at any time is good enough. "How about Main street at noon?" But if our intention is to grow, to develop some real depth to our relationship, we will give serious thought to the appropriate time for the battle. This does not preclude a skirmish at an awkward time. Perhaps when having dinner with some friends, a few sharp words are exchanged but discretion is a wise move.

Self control is an important part of a good fight. Self control will allow us to choose the best time to deal with the issues that have caused the tension to rise to a level that needs addressing. The emphasis is on _self_.

Paul goes on in Ephesians 4: 28 and says, *"He who has been stealing must steal no more, but must work, doing something useful with his own hands, that he may have something to share with those in need."*. Now you may be thinking, "What in the world does this have to do with conflict in our marriage?" The principle Paul is addressing is be ready with a positive solution. Paul talks about someone stealing, his positive solution, "Let him labor." He could go on and on about what's wrong with stealing, why it's wrong, why the person who is stealing is bad, but he doesn't. He gets right to a positive solution to the problem. It's not unusual for any of us, in the heat of an argument to belabor our point. We want to make sure the other person hears what we're saying. Meanwhile, we never get around to a positive solution. Or if we do, the other person is so worn out from the barrage of what they had done wrong; they had no emotional energy left to hear the solution we presented.

If we have a legitimate criticism or complaint against our mate, especially if it's something we know is going to hurt, then let's be prepared with a positive supportive solution that can take some of the sting out of the wound. Condemnation without hope crushes. And the purpose of the argument is not that we win, but that our marriage becomes stronger.

Paul continues in Ephesians 4:29, *"Do not let any unwholesome talk come out of your mouth . . ."* The principle he gives us is, weigh our words and watch our tone. It's amazing how easy it is for this to get away from us. In the heat of an exchange, before we know it, we say something that crushes the spirit of our mate. If our agenda is to make sure we win, cutting deeps wounds in the spirit of our mate is not an issue. If we're looking for a long term growing relationship, Paul's counsel is worth heeding.

This is a tough one. When we want to make our point what do we do? Get louder. But you actually say more when you say less and say it softer. The louder we get, the less others hear. Paul's choice of word here for "unwholesome" means rotten or putrid. It would certainly include profanity or swearing, but notice how much further Paul takes us, *but only what is helpful for building others up according to their needs, that it may benefit those who listen.* Honestly now, how many of us when we're in the heat of contention stop and think: "I wonder if these next few words will be a source of tremendous encouragement and edification to this thick skinned, narrow minded, self serving pig headed person." Know what Paul is talking about? Tactfulness. And tactfulness carries with it a healthy respect for the person we are trying to communicate with.

My wife and I came from two entirely different backgrounds when it came to resolving conflict in our marriage. My wife's parents are very disciplined people and very selective of how they expressed themselves. I came from a background where my father was a *rager*. On any given occasion he could explode and everybody around him got hit with the shrapnel. So our first few battlefield encounters were pretty ugly. It didn't take me very long to figure out how destructive my approach could be. I had never seen someone actually use, self control in the middle of an argument. After awhile I began to learn that not saying everything I was thinking was a good thing. Eventually my wife and I established a personal guideline for me, "weigh your words." That was thirty five years ago. They are still words I live by to this day. For our conflict to bring depth to our relationship we need to choose our time, we need to weigh our words and choose the right weapons.

Paul goes on in Ephesians 4:31, *"Get rid of all bitterness, rage and anger, brawling and slander, along with every form of malice."* The principle is no attacking in public. When we attack in public, our malice is showing. We can attack people in "malice or bitterness" in two different ways: Bold open criticism in front of friend family or neighbors, and some of us are very good at this. Bringing all the dirty laundry out for all to see. Or subtle cutting sarcasm, a game many a couple plays. Everyone else is laughing, but between the two of you, the joke hurts. Husbands I know it's clever to make fun of the way your wife does house work, but do you know that is one of her primary sources of self esteem. Wives you know his getting bald or putting on weight or having some gray hair may make for a great joke, but what of his self image? Whether its open criticism or cynical sarcasm, either hurts just as much.

Here's the last rule for a good fight, it comes from Ephesians 4:32, *"Be kind and compassionate to one another, forgiving one another just as in Christ God forgave you."* The principle is when it's over, help clean up the mess. Have you ever noticed those few minutes after a heated exchange and you're looking for the right words. You're searching the memories banks trying to find some way to get this monster back under control. Maybe you blew it, maybe they blew it – you just want to wrap it up?

The words we're looking for are, "I'm sorry I blew up." Jesus taught in Matthew 6:14, *"If you forgive others for the wrongs they do to you, your Father in heaven will forgive you. But if you don't forgive others, your Father will not forgive your sins."* We may not be asking forgiveness for bringing up a subject that really needed addressing. We may very well be asking forgiveness for the *way* we brought the matter up, or the time when we chose to bring it up.

Cleaning up the mess means taking the time to check for wounds and unintended scaring. Instead of just walking off and the wounded can take care of themselves, we stay and look for ways to bring some healing to the person we say we love. This calls for a tremendous amount of self control. But it has the potential to bring a lot of depth into a marriage.

For a productive fight, lay the ground rules, and start with, "I trust you, and I trust this argument will draw us closer together, let's roll up sleeves and let's get started" Can you start that way, probably not, but it's still an attitude we can hold on to. It's a matter of what we hope to accomplish in our quarrel.

Have you ever thought about the words that can help stop a fight in progress? A few simple, heart felt words like: *"I'm sorry."* *"I was wrong."* *" Please forgive me."* *"I love you."* Will these few words stop every skirmish? No. But they are a great place to begin.

Heated discussions, arguments, fights are a part of married life. Few are the couples who never have such disagreements. God understood and gave us a plan to take what could be a very negative, even divisive situation in our marriage and turn it into something that can actually improve our marriage. But it starts with us; having the desire that even when facing some really tough issues, even when our quarrel went further than we intended, there is a benefit that our relationship can receive. The benefit is growing some depth to our relationship and even learning a lesson about ourselves from every heated exchange. And once the conflict begins, let's play by the rules.

Worksheet
Playing By The Rules

1. Do we want our conflict to help us develop more depth to our relationship?

2. Are we both committed to being honest and respecting one another?

3. When we have had an argument in the past, have we chosen our weapons wisely?

4. Has there ever been a time when I have crushed your spirit?

5. Are we committed to confiding in one another and letting the past be the past?

6. How have we done in choosing the right time for a battle?

7. Have I been ready with a positive solution in arguments we have had?

8. How are we doing in weighing our words and watching our tone?

9. Are we making good choices as to where we have our arguments?

10. Are we staying around after the skirmish to help clean up? Do we find ways of reconciliation after a heated argument?

Chapter Six

The Day Is Finally Here

So the day you've been waiting for, planning for, hoping for is just around the corner. This ought to be a time to enjoy every moment of every activity. But for the most part, the days leading up to the wedding day seem to be filled with a lot of stress. So let's deal with something right up front. The day of your wedding, the day when everything should be perfect, won't be.

Someone needs to say it out loud, so I'll be the one. Something will go wrong; someone will forget their cue, you'll drop the ring and it will roll to the back of the sanctuary, the ring bearer will refuse to walk with the flower girl, or Uncle Ed will have too much punch and start singing old Frank Sinatra show tunes like he did at Aunt Betty's funeral. I don't know what it will be, but it will be. And the bottom line is, it's OK. You can live with it and later even wear the misfortunes as a badge of accomplishment. Because there's a long list of things that are more important than the perfect wedding day. Let's take a second and remember them:

- You're getting married to the person you love.
- You're family, even Uncle Ed, will all be together.
- You live in a land and at a time when you have the freedom to get married.
- The people who matter most to you are all pulling for you, they want everything to go perfectly and they'll role with the punches if it doesn't.
- Even if the pastor forgets "Will you have this person...." you'll remind him.

There are a lot of things that can go wrong. But there are a thousand more things that can and will go right. So relax, make up your mind in advance that you will enjoy Uncle Ed's rendition of "New York, New York" and just hope to God the video doesn't show up on America's Wildest Weddings. You see your wedding day is something you plan; it is not something you can control. If I had a nickel for every flower girl who changed her mind just before walking down the aisle at the final event, I could finally buy a Lamborghini (well that's not completely true, maybe just a Porsche)but the mistakes are something we can live with.

Having said all that, we should recognize that weddings are not for the feint of heart. For many couples, planning their wedding is their first event-planning experience and there's a lot of expectation to make the day as perfect as it can be. Even with the best of planning there will be some mistakes but it doesn't have to be a nightmare. There are a few things we can do to minimize stress and make planning this special day a little less stressful.

First of all we need to start by knowing where the finances will be coming from. In the past throughout most of the country, the groom or their family have been expected to pay for the rehearsal dinner, while the bride's family takes care of financing the wedding and reception. In various cultures, even within the U.S. who handles the finances are handled differently.

There's an interesting history to the term *honeymoon*. As best as we can tell the phrase originated more than two-thousand years ago in old Babylon. It had to do when the father of the bride would give the groom a supply of celebration drink made from honey (and normally with high alcohol content) enough celebration drink that would last for thirty days, or to the next moon phase, at which time the celebration would be officially ended and the newly wed couple, their friends and everyone else got on with life. Thus the word honeymoon became the term to describe a couples celebration time. But sometimes it's alright to break with tradition. It's important to talk with our families early on to decide who's paying for what.

In the past fifteen to twenty years, I have noticed more and more couples who cover the expenses themselves. Sometimes because of their financial ability and other times because it helps minimize expectations and stress. Keep in mind that if we rely on others to pay for our wedding, we may be setting the stage for more stress. And the reasoning is very simple, the more people invest in something financially, the more control they feel they should have in the matter. It's not unusual for brides and grooms to differ with their families over various parts of the wedding day like facilities, the music, the seating arrangements, the flowers, the dresses, and even the menu. If you can afford to cover the costs yourself, it solves a lot of problems. If our family is going to help with expenses, or cover all the expenses, a meeting of the minds before we get too far in the planning is extremely helpful. This meeting usually helps determine *who* is actually deciding *what* in the planning stages.

After addressing the issue of finances, we can get down to the nitty-gritty of the actual wedding ceremony. One of the best things we can do is make sure there's time for advanced planning. Think about this for a second, there are at least fifteen different cues that must be given (and received) just to get the ceremony started; a cue to the organist or sound person to start the music, cue the ushers where to seat the guests, when to seat the guests, cue the grandparents, the parents, the ring bearer, the flower girl, the first bridesmaid, the second, the third, cue the groomsmen, the groom, the pastor and the bride. Then make sure that everyone knows where to start and where to finish. And we haven't even said, "Dearly beloved we are gathered here today to join this man and this woman in holy matrimony!"

Having sat with hundreds of couples during just a portion of their planning process, I'm getting to the point where I can pretty well tell in advance who's going to have a smooth ceremony and who is open to a lot of disappointment. All because of the lack of attention to details. It would be foolish for a bride to rush into a wedding gown store, look at one or two dresses and then, without trying any gown on, just pick a dress and hope that it fits. Most of the time a bride takes her time, goes with her mother or family, tries on several, talks about design, style, and comfort. A bride gives the choosing of her dress a lot of thought. Why? Because it's important to her, it's her wedding dress. The wedding day will go much more smoothly if we take the time to plan the day. I'm not talking the planning that went into storming the beaches of Normandy, just attention to some of the details.

In the addendum there is a short schedule for planning the wedding day. It is intended only as a place to start, you may want to add more details to the schedule. Especially if there is family come in from out of town, or transportation needs to be arranged for someone in the wedding party.

Please allow me to add just a quick observation here. The majority of time the grooms I meet with are unsure what their part is in the planning. So I often hear, "Whatever she wants is alright with me." But guys this is your day too. Talk with your bride about the details, even if some aspect of the ceremony isn't that interesting to you, exchange ideas with your future wife and become a sounding board for her. I cannot count the number of grooms I have "nudged" into being more involved with the planning process, only to be told later how much more they enjoyed the ceremony and it is a memory they will hold onto for a lifetime.

The biggest issue in planning the wedding day is people. How to move people from one spot to the next and how to get them to stop on that spot. One of the best ways to insure that movement will go smoothly on the wedding day is to go to the facility where the ceremony will be conducted. Most facilities, churches in particular, have wedding coordinators. These are your best friends! Pick their brains; ask them about how things work, what are some mistakes they could help you keep from doing. They can give you little pointers like a side room is too small for ten groomsmen, be careful walking down the steps from the podium in a long dress, and a long list of pointers. These little insights make a huge difference in making the wedding day everything we had hoped for.

Music is an important part of the wedding ceremony. Just as a recommendation, before we say yes to anyone singing or playing, go and listen to them perform. This includes church musicians. Especially church musicians. There are many church organists and pianists who do a great job playing for the congregation on a Sunday morning, and then somehow turn the wedding march into a funeral drudge. If we're going to use the church organist, meet with them several months in advance and listen to them play the music selections you have in mind. The same goes with any vocalists that may "volunteer" to sing on your wedding day. Aunt Libby sounds great in the shower, but she really has a tough time reaching those high notes on "The Wedding Song". It's for this reason many couples opt on using pre-recorded sound (sound tracks) versus live music.

Just a quick note on using pre-recorded music and sound systems. Meet with the sound person several months in advance. Make sure to meet with the actual person who will be running the equipment the day of the ceremony. And it doesn't hurt to bring with you someone who will be present the day of the ceremony who will know which track goes where in the ceremony and has a good grasp on the cues for each track. Many a ceremony has derailed because the sound person got sick and a substitute had to step in. It's amazing how much music affects the flow of the ceremony. And I know that you may love to have a head banging, heavy metal song as your exist song, but try to remember grandma is sitting right in front of the speakers and she's still getting over that heart condition problem. Moderation will go a long way in allowing the music selection to compliment the ceremony, versus becoming the vocal point of the ceremony. Remember, the goal is our family and friends would give all their attention to the bride and her groom, not to the peripherals' of the ceremony.

The meeting with the officiate of the ceremony; whether a pastor or other officiate is really the boiling down time to the many ideas that have been floating around as you plan for your wedding day. Each state has a different list of "acceptable" officiates allowed to conduct a wedding. The addendum has some additional information about license and officiates. Make sure to check with the County Clerk where the ceremony will be held to meet whatever requirements they might have.

The meeting with the pastor or officiate is more than just the details to the ceremony. As a pastor I try to open up issues a couple may have overlooked in preparing themselves for the day, as well as address issues on what to include or not include in the actual ceremony. One of the most important parts of this meeting is to decide on the wedding vows. This is normally the last thing on a couples list of "important". But I assure you that time spent addressing the choice of words now, will save a lot of awkwardness when you're standing in front of two-hundred people.

An outline I have used on many occasions looks something like this, with some additional comments for your use:

Paul & Elizabeth Smith   November 11, 2005

Prelude Music	Guests Seated	1:55
Summer Song	Grandparents Enter	2:00
A Time For Us	Parents enter	2:05
The Wedding Song	Bridesmaid enter Groomsmen enter Ring Bearer/Flower Girl	2:09
Wedding March	Father & Bride Stop at mark	2:16
Music Ends	Pastor's Opening	

To Congregation: Please be seated. **Dearly beloved we've gathered in the presence of family and friends to join this man and this woman in Holy matrimony, which is an honorable estate. Who gives this woman to be married to this man?** (*Father replies, Her mother and I do.*)

Music Begins *Our Day*	*(Raises Bride's veil and gives her a kiss.* *Groom steps forward Father places her hand in* *hand of groom and is seated. Bride and Groom* *step up to podium.)*

Pastor's Sermonette *(Be sure and find out what the pastor is going to say and how long it's going to take to say it)* This relationship is built upon love. Nothing else will weather the storm. I Corinthians 13 tell us: Love is patient, love is kind. It does not envy, it does not boast, it is not proud. It is not rude, it is not self-seeking, it is not easily angered, and it keeps no record of wrong. Love does not delight in evil but rejoices with the truth. It always protects, always trusts, always hopes, always preserves. Love never fails. Into this relationship the two of you come now to be joined.

Vows: *(These are the vows that the couple shares with the congregation. Basically a statement saying, "we're here to get married.")* Elizabeth will you have this man to be your lawfully wedded husband, to live together in the holy estate of matrimony, to love, honor, and cherish till death do you part?

Paul will you have this woman to be your lawfully wedded wife, to live together in the holy estate of matrimony, to love, honor, and cherish till death do you part?

Before these witnesses and before God would you commit your love to one another but repeating after me: *(These are the couples vows, they mean nothing to the congregation, they are intended to be shared only between the two)*

I Paul . . . take thee Elizabeth . . . to be my wedded wife . . . to have and to hold . . . from this day forward . . . for better or for worse . . . for richer or poorer . . . in sickness and in health . . . to love and to cherish . . . till death do us part . . . I pledge you my love . . . *(Cue vocalist to get into position)*

I Elizabeth . . . take thee Paul . . . to be my wedded husband . . . to have and to hold . . . from this day forward . . . for better or for worse . . . for richer or poorer . . . in sickness and in health . . . to love and to cherish . . . till death do us part . . . I pledge you my love . . . *(Music begins, vocalist sings)*

Song   *Butterflies*   *(Couple remains)*

Pastor: Paul would you further seal these vows by giving and receiving of a ring? *(Paul responses I will)* Taking this ring and using it as the emblem of your purity and unending love for Elizabeth place it on the ring finger of your bride and repeat after me ---

(While placing the ring on her ring finger) With this ring . . . I thee wed . . . With all my hearts affections . . . I commit myself to you . . .

Elizabeth would you further seal these vows by giving and receiving of a ring? *(Elizabeth responses I will)* Taking this ring and using it as the emblem of your purity and unending love for Paul place it on the ring finger of your groom and repeat after me ---

(While placing the ring on his ring finger) With this ring . . . I thee wed . . . With all my hearts affections . . . I commit myself to you . . .
(Taking the hands of each, the pastor addresses the couple) Let's talk about the importance of these rings . . . *(Pastor steps back – cue for vocalist)*

To begin your journey as husband and wife, the lighting of the Unity Candle is your statement of the combining of both of your families, the love they have shared, into preparing you to start your lives' together. *(Pastor steps back, couple steps forward to table, vocalist begins, couple remains till last stanza)*

Song   *The Lords Prayer*   *(Couple in place)*

Now by the authority of the state of California, I pronounce you husband & wife, you may kiss your bride/groom. *(And then the moment we've been waiting for.)* May I introduce to you Mr.& Mrs. Paul & Elizabeth Smith

Music   *Wedding March*   *(Bride/Groom lead out, wedding party follows, all parents follow)*

The wedding party and parents assemble in the   2:55
vestibule for greetings and introductions.
Wedding guests assemble in reception hall
(Have refreshment available)

Photographer gets into position for wedding photos.   3:15

Wedding party arrives at reception hall   4:00
(Have DJ ready for intros)

Your wedding reception is a great time to celebrate. In the addendum are some recommendations to help the "Best Man" conduct the toasts. Be prepared at the reception to spend very little time relaxing. After the many toasts, the couples dance, and the father/daughter dance, the couple now gets to thank and visit each guest in the room. This is your assigned duty. Don't miss a single person, especially Aunt Rose, she will remember she was overlooked for the next 500 years!

All kidding aside, enjoy your reception and your family. Yeah, your feet are sore, so take your shoes off. And stay away from the alcohol till afterwards, we want the guests to get a little foggy in the brain, not you. These are the people who care about you. I have watched many couples invite hundreds of friends and families to their wedding, only to have seventy-five people actually show up. So take the time to express your appreciation for these people who cared enough about you to take an afternoon and spend it on you.

And after all the music is over, after all the guests have left, go tell your parents thanks. I know it sounds corny, but they just watched their little girl get handed over to this big gorilla and they need some reassuring. And your wedding party could use a few "thanks" as well. They stayed on their marks and even the flower girl gave in and held hands with the ring bearer.

By the way, the flower girl thinks the bride is like a princess. And to have the princess actually kneel down and talk to her, would make her day. If you take the time, this will be a memory that will be with all of your family for a lot of years ahead.

There's been a lot of commotion in this all important day. Maybe things went perfectly; maybe Uncle Ed did what you feared he was going to do. It's still OK. What really matters is the two of you. Laugh about what went wrong, and then hold each other like you've never been able to do before this moment, as husband and wife.

Worksheet
Preparing For Our Day

1. What kind of wedding do we want? Formal, less formal?

2. What kind of music do we want to play?

3. Do we want any special music, or vocalists?

4. How big a guest list are we going to have? What can we afford?

5. Where will we hold the ceremony? The reception?

6. What are some family issues we need to address? How can we honor our families in our day?

7. Who will make up our wedding party?

8. How will we finance our wedding day?

9. What are some aspects of the ceremony that are important to us? What special things would we like to have in the ceremony?

10. What else would make this day, "our day"?

Chapter Seven

Keeping The Spark Alive

So we've walked down the aisle, we exchanged the rings, our Moms sat crying in the front row, we even survived the reception afterwards, and the honeymoon was incredible. Now it's time for the tough work of marriage. And I know that it sounds strange, but hear me out. The tough part of marriage is keeping the flame alive. Keeping that spark in your heart, so that every time you're apart for a few days, it seems as though there's a piece of you missing. We don't talk about this very much. We think it's just automatic, now that we're married, of course we'll stay in love.

I have a standing agreement with every couple that I marry. The agreement is, beyond whatever honorarium they give me, whether it's $10 or $1000, the couple agrees to a second honorarium. The second honorarium is in the form of a privilege. The privilege is, after the ceremony is finished, after all the commotion calms down, I take the outline of their ceremony from my Bible. The outline that has who sang where, when we lit the candles and even the exact words to the vows that were exchanged. And I place that outline in my file, along with the hundreds of others wedding outlines I have kept over the years. And I keep that outline on file, until I hear one day that the couple, who stood before me and said all those nice things, is going through some tough times. They are even thinking of breaking up, of getting a divorce.

It's at that point I collect the second part of my honorarium. I go to the file, find the outline of the ceremony. Take the outline to their house, where I knock on the front door. Of course, they're peeking through the curtains and they'll act like they're not home. That doesn't slow me down. Right there, on their front porch, I take the outline from my Bible and I start reading, loudly. **"Dearly beloved we are gathered here today in the sight of God and the presence of these witnesses . . . "** And I just keep going till either they open the door or the neighbors call the police. They normally open the door.

Then we sit down at the kitchen table and I ask two questions, "Did you mean what you said when I ask you whether you would love, honor and cherish 'til death do you part?" And I always get a yes. Then the second question is, "Do you mean them now?" Which brings out a flood of issues why they have (the most often used phrase is) fallen out of love. And then we begin to sort through all the issues that have led them to this point in their marriage.

Over the years I have never had a single couple turn down this part of my honorarium. In fact I have had several couples call me to "collect" on the offer I make them. I have always found it interesting why no one ever turns me down. The best I can tell is they don't think they will ever reach a point that a divorce would ever cross their mind. But it does and for all sorts of reasons.

Malachi 2:16 says that God hates divorce. It does not say that he hates people who have divorced. And I can see why God hates divorce, divorce is painful. Even the person who wins, still loses, still hurts, still cries alone about what they had hoped they would have in a marriage and it didn't happen. Divorce or separation is probably the last thought on our mind as we prepare for tying the knot. But it helps to have a game plan in place so that we can say we did everything possible to keep that day from coming. In fact, I've found that to have a game plan in place not only keeps that day from coming, it also gives us some markers to know how we are doing in keeping the spark alive. The game plan is found in Philippians 2:2 which says, *"If you have any encouragement from being united with Christ, if any comfort from his love, if any fellowship with the Spirit, if any tenderness and compassion, then make my joy complete by being like-minded, having the same love, being one in spirit and purpose. Do nothing out of selfish ambition or vain conceit, but in humility consider others better than yourselves. Each of you should look not only to your own interests, but also to the interests of others."* In these few verses God provides for us a game plan to help not only keep the spark alive, but to having a satisfying and fulfilling marriage.

From this verse and other passage of scripture, the best I can tell regarding God's idea of marriage is that it would include unity, comfort, fellowship, tenderness and compassion. Which makes a pretty good "short list" for describing a healthy marriage; two people who are united, providing comfort to one another, along with meaningful fellowship, through expressions of tenderness and compassion. And I know guys, that the list sound so, "fluffy". But if we're looking to keep the spark alive for more than the first seven years, there will be times the two of you will have to stand united (especially if you have a two-year-old in your home), on many occasion providing comfort to our marriage partner and in the process giving and receiving the benefits of sharing life (fellowship) while expressing our love and appreciation through tenderness and compassion.

But this passage in Philippians also give us a game plan on how to keep the spark alive while our marriage develops the roots that will keep it a long and fulfilling relationship. The first part of the plan is to be *like minded*. This would best be described as thinking on the same wave length. There will always be a difference in our thinking, we are two separate people and we think differently. The idea of being like minded would reflect a choice. Choosing to think in a similar fashion as the other person. In fact it's probably something you've already been doing without being aware of it.

When you talk about your ceremony, who is going to do what, chances are good that if you were in separate rooms you would come up with two separate lists as to who is doing what. But as you sit together, talk about things, hear the other person say that would like this or like that, you choose to change your thinking. Yes, I know this is not a perfect illustration because I have sat with couples when there's not an agreement on who does what. But we do understand the principle involved.

If you would have told me the first year of my marriage, that the day would come that I could tell you what my wife was thinking, I would have called you crazy. After thirty-five years I have a pretty good idea what she thinks about a whole host of issues, including what does not go well with the curtains and throw pillows on the couch.

The goal is not that we would be identical in our thinking. That would be boring. Instead the idea is that two people would choose to think alike, and to exchange ideas so that our differences would compliment one another. This requires some healthy communicating.

I have always been fascinated that two people, prior to their wedding day could have so much to talk about. In fact spend hours in conversation, but six months into their marriage their conversations have boiled down to a few words a day. A very interesting study conducted in 2004 revealed that the average American couple watched forty-six hours of television in a week. But only spent twenty-three minutes in meaningful conversation in a week. In a week, not a day, a week. And we wonder why we don't seem to communicate very well.

If we start out with a game plan that says we intend to keep this spark alive and well for a long time, we will need to pay attention to our communication and being like minded. There will be times when good conversation might be difficult. It doesn't need to be a forced thing. Think about what you talk about now? Everything! Why? Because we are genuinely interested in getting to know the other person. We <u>want</u> to know about their day, what went good and what went bad. This is a choice we need to hang on to.

The second part of our game plan is found in the words, *have the same love.* You may be familiar with the three types of love that are found in the Bible. The first is *eros*, from which we get the word erotic. This is purely a sexual love. It is based solely on "What will this person do for me? How will they meet my needs?" IF a relationship is based solely on sexual satisfaction, the day will come very soon where the sex just isn't good enough any more, then we will need to find the next big thrill. The second kind of love found in the Bible is *phileo*, which is best described as a brotherly love. Philadelphia is rightly called the city of brotherly love. This kind of love is best expressed by our regard of, or our appreciation for another person. And the third type of love in the Bible is *agape*, which means love without limits. It is the kind of love God demonstrated by giving His Son for us. It is the highest quality of love.

Now the passage in Philippians calls us to have the same *agape* for one another. And we might think this strange, but there is an application. Part of the marriage relationship is obviously sexual, but a big part of the relationship is non-sexual. I have even heard couples talk about how they were first friends before they became lovers. God's plan for keeping the spark alive calls for us to develop the kind of love that is the highest quality of love. As we begin our relationship there may be a high level of eros. That is not unusual. But the goal is to turn our love into something that will develop, even grow over time.

My wife and I have a standing joke. Well she thinks it's a joke and I keep telling her that it's not. She will tease me by telling me, "I have always loved you more." To which my reply is, "You're absolutely right." For her to stay around through those early years of our marriage when I was fumbling around, trying to find out what real love for my wife looked like, yes she has always loved me more. And I am so glad she did. But now, in the words of Captain Jack Sparrow, *"I'm catching up!"*

The third part of God's game plan is *being one in purpose*. We could say, we're singing off the same page. Here we have to decide in what direction our marriage is going to go. Is our marriage just about having a license so we can have sex? Is our marriage partnership about accumulating stuff? What is the ultimate objective of our marriage?

None of us would start a job with a company without knowing what our job description involved. Or go into surgery if the doctor's reason for operating was, "I just want to look around a little?" And the chances are very good that you have already talked about this, perhaps indirectly, but you've talked about it. Whenever you talked about "why", why are we getting married? You began exploring the purpose for your marriage.

Over time the purpose will change. At various seasons of your marriage different purpose will take the lead. In some seasons the purpose will be more on accomplishing; getting through school, or starting the new career, or buying a new home. At other seasons it will be focused more on putting down roots; having a family, choosing not to accept the promotion that takes you to a new town. The purposes will change; the key is that both partners are supporting those changes. There will be times when it will take some long conversations to hear each other out, but to keep the spark alive those conversations are worth having.

Which brings us to the next part of God's game plan, *do nothing out of selfish ambition.* We could say, fight the need of self. Checking our agenda on why we are doing what we are doing. Even when we're arguing, the thought needs to be in the back of our mind, "Why am I doing this? Why am I making this such an issue?" As one couple told me one time, "When we really get heated about something, we ask each other, 'Is this the hill you want to die on?'" That sounds pretty encouraging doesn't it?

One of my favorite stories about selfish ambition in marriage comes from a time when I was a very young pastor. I had just started serving at a small rural church and one of the Elders was a man named Sam. You couldn't ask for a better guy. He cared for people, loved God, thoroughly enjoyed learning the Bible, always sought what was best for the congregation, and was a good leader. One day Sam told me his story, well actually he and his wife Pat's story.

For the first seventeen years of their marriage Pat was a church going Christian and Sam was not. In fact he did everything he could to discouragement Pat from going to church, including planning family events on Sunday so she would have to stay home rather than go to church. Sam was constantly giving Pat a hard time about going to church and believing all that "crap they try and feed you." In fact on one occasion Sam literally threw the pastor out of the house when the pastor stopped by for a visit.

As I sat listening to this, I could not believe my ears. The Sam in this story was in no way the Sam that I knew. So I asked Sam, "Why did you do that? Why give Pat such a hard time about being a Christian?" To which his reply was, "Pat was the only Christian I had ever known. I mean someone who was really a Christian. And I figured if I could break her, I was off the hook. So I did everything I could think of, but she wouldn't break. Eventually I knew that she was right."

Sam went on to tell of the day when he finally knew she was right and he had no excuses left. Pat had put up with all he could dish out for seventeen years and did not break. One Sunday morning, as Pat was getting ready for church, Sam asked, "Guess you're going to church again?" "Yes" was Pat's reply. "Can I go with you?" Sam asked. "Why, so you can throw the pastor out a window?" Pat asked. "Nope, just to go with you." was Sam's response. To which he did. Eight months later Sam was baptized. I met Sam five years after that and he is one of the kindest most gentle men I have ever served with. Sam would be the first to tell you that he struggled at great length with his own selfish ambition

That passage in Philippians goes on to say, in *humility consider others better than yourself.* Boy there's a challenge for us. Not only does God want us to fight our own self interests, He wants us to choose to put others ahead of ourselves. There's a word that we use to describe this, the word is consideration. Why do we hold the door open for someone at the grocery store whose arms are full and can't reach the door handle? Out of consideration. This is an incredible quality found in too few couples.

As I have counseled couples of all ages, I have watched the full spectrum of consideration. All the way from "get the door yourself", to going the second and third mile in showing consideration to their partner. I have also seen the difference it makes in the marriage relationship. Guess which couples have the healthier marriage, the ones showing less or more consideration? This is part of the game plan, we can put into action before we even have the ceremony. And it becomes a part of our family culture that gets passed on to the next generation.

There is one last part in this game plan, It's found in those few words; *look not only to your own interests but also to the interests of others.* We would call this having a balanced life. By our very nature we are mindful of our self interests. Though for some of us there may be things in our life that keep us from having a healthy self interest. But we should notice God is not calling us to a relationship that is harmful to ourselves.

On one occasion Jesus was asked which of the commandments was the greatest commandment? To which His reply was, *"Love the Lord your God with all your heart, soul and mind. And the second is like unto the first, Love your neighbor as yourself."* If we don't have a healthy self appreciation, we will most definitely have a harmful relationship with others. We will never be able to adequately love others without loving ourselves. Here's where our being of one purpose comes into play. We need to be open with our mate about things that have happened in our life. There's a lot of strength to be found in allowing another person to really know who we are. If our purpose is to keep the spark not only alive, but burning brightly for the years ahead, looking to the interests of each other is a critical part of God's plan. Now take your time learning and opening up to each other. You have time to work on things. Not everything has to be addressed overnight.

Solomon had an idea in mind, thousands of years ago when he collected the wise sayings we read in Ecclesiastes. Where we read in Ecclesiastes 9:9, *"Enjoy life with your wife, whom you love, all the days of this life. . . "* The word for "enjoy" carries with it the idea of a continual celebration. The party never ends, as we say. To keep the spark alive, enjoy one another. And to really enjoy one another, we all need some help.

Perhaps you've heard someone say, "It takes two people to make a marriage work." Well I disagree; I'm convinced it takes three, to make a healthy fulfilling marriage. On the stand that holds my camera in place when I'm taking those crazy family pictures at the birthday parties, there are three legs. Now two legs can hold up the camera, but I get a lot sharper picture when I use all three legs. The real power to bringing lasting healthy change in our marriage is the person of Jesus Christ. I know, you expect a pastor to say that. But I've seen what His presence can do. In each phase of a healthy marriage, He can provide the strength and insight to help us keep that spark alive.

A study conducted amongst married couples in America in 2005, revealed that only three percent every make it to fifty years together as a couple. A big percentage because of death. But a huge percentage because they just couldn't keep the spark burning. Our goal is to hand off to the generation that follows a great legacy. The picture of two people who for all their married life, genuinely and honestly cared for one another.

Worksheet
Keeping The Spark Alive

1. How do we do in compromising on things?

2. Why are we getting married?

3. What is the best illustration of a healthy marriage we have seen?

4. Do we need any help in some area of our relationship?

5. Are we keeping a healthy balance in our self interest?

6. How would we describe the phase we are in?

7. What will we look like in 20 years?

8. Do we intend to say, "Till death do we part"?

9. How important is our "faith" to our marriage?

10. Would we take Dave up on his offer?

Addendum: Useful Tool

Marriage License Information

Wedding license requirement vary according to state, and even counties within some states. The requirements for a marriage license in California are:

You do not need to be a California resident to marry in California. Only an unmarried male and an unmarried female may marry in California. Marriage by proxy is NOT allowed in California. Family Code, Section 420(a) requires the bride, groom, marriage officiate and witness if applicable, be physically present together in the same location for the marriage to be performed.

Blood tests are NOT required to obtain a marriage license in California. Both parties must appear in person and bring valid picture identification to the County Clerk's Office to apply for a marriage license in California. Valid picture identification is one that contains a photograph, date of birth, and an issue and expiration date, such as a state issued identification card, drivers license, passport, military identification, etc. Some counties may also require a copy of your birth certificate.

If you have been married before, you will need to know the specific date your last marriage ended, and how it ended (Death, Dissolution, Divorce or Nullity). Some counties may require a copy of the final judgment if your previous marriage ended by dissolution or nullity.

Marriage licenses are valid for 90 days from the date of issuance. If you do not get married within 90 days, the license will no longer be valid. **You must purchase a new license.**

Many County Clerks in California perform civil marriage ceremonies in their offices. For further information regarding civil marriage ceremonies, please contact the County Clerk's Office directly to see if they provide this service.

Marriage License Information (Con't)

California Family Code, Section 400 states the persons authorized to solemnize marriage ceremonies in California are as follows:

A priest, minister, or rabbi of any religious denomination. A judge or retired judge, commissioner of civil marriages or retired commissioner of civil marriages, commissioner or retired commissioner, or assistant commissioner of a court of record in this state. A judge or magistrate who has resigned from office.

Any of the following judges or magistrates of the United States:

> A justice or retired justice of the United States Supreme Court.
> A judge or retired judge of a court of appeals, a district court, or a court created by an act of Congress the judges of which are entitled to hold office during good behavior.
> A judge or retired judge of a bankruptcy court or a tax court.
> A United States magistrate or retired magistrate.
> A legislator or constitutional officer of this state or a member of Congress who represents a district within this state, while that person holds office.

All fees and hours of issuance for a marriage license may vary by county.

The person solemnizing the marriage must return the original marriage license to the County Clerk or County Recorder as applicable within 10 days of the date of the ceremony. Addresses should be on the county site.

You will NOT receive a copy of your marriage license after you have been married unless you request and pay for a certified copy from the County Clerk or County Recorder as applicable.

Marriage License Information (Con't)

Who May Perform Marriages Abroad

American diplomatic and consular officers are NOT permitted to perform marriages. Marriages abroad are almost always performed by local (foreign) civil or religious officials. As a rule, marriages are not performed on the premises of an American embassy or consulate. The validity of marriages abroad is not dependent upon the presence of an American diplomatic or consular officer, but upon adherence to the laws of the country where the marriage is performed. Consular officers may authenticate foreign marriage documents. The fee for authentication of a document is $32.00.

Validity of Marriages Abroad

In general, marriages which are legally performed and valid abroad are also legally valid in the United States. Inquiries regarding the validity of a marriage abroad should be directed to the attorney general of the state in the U.S. where the parties to the married live.

Foreign Laws and Procedures

The embassy or tourist information bureau of the country in which the marriage is to be performed is the best source of information about marriage in that country. Some general information on marriage in a limited number of countries can be obtained from Overseas Citizens Services, Dept. of State, Washington, DC 20520. In addition, American embassies and consulates abroad frequently have information about marriage in the country in which they are located.

Residence & Documentation Requirements

Marriages abroad are subject to the residency requirements of the country in which the marriage is to be performed. There is almost always a lengthy waiting period. Most countries require that a valid U.S. passport be presented. In addition, birth certificates, divorce decrees, and death certificates are frequently required. Some countries require that the documents presented to the marriage registrar first be authenticated in the United States by a consular official of that country. This process can be time consuming and expensive.

Planning Calendar

6-12 Months Prior
- Choose the kind of wedding you will have, date & time.
- Discuss the budget, and who will pay for what.
- Make arrangements with the officiator.
- Reserve the wedding and reception locations.
- Select your wedding dress, veil and accessories.
- Choose the bridesmaids, groomsmen, and ushers.
- Have black/white photo sitting for announcements.
- Send announcements of your engagement to your fiancé's and your local and hometown newspapers.
- Meet with the florist, photographer, caterer, and D.J. to discuss budgets and options.
- Discuss the guest list with fiancé and families.
- Contact a rental coordinator for reserving equipment.
- Discuss honeymoon and reservations. (Groom traditionally makes honeymoon arrangements.)
- Arrange for time off work, if necessary.
- Buy wedding planner, store notes, invitations, gifts, and thank-you notes.

4-6 Months Prior
- Plan new living arrangements and home furnishings.
- Select and register wedding gifts and patterns.
- Select color scheme, choose music
- Order bridesmaid's dresses and accessories.
- Contact men's specialist wear for men's attire.
- Have parents select attire.
- Order invitations, announcements, programs, napkins, matchbooks, and personal stationery.
- Arrange for physical examinations, dental appts.

2 Months Prior
- Choose and order wedding bands and engraving.
- Choose & order wedding and groom's cakes.
- Check state/county marriage license requirements.
- Plan ceremony, reception, menus, and timetables.
- Plan rehearsal dinner, and bridesmaids' luncheon.
- Complete guest list and address invitations.
- Make arrangements for lodging for out-of-town guests.
- Purchase gifts for attendants and groom.
- Plan reception seating, if necessary.

Wedding Day Schedule

The following chart will help you with the essentials; the spaces between each item will let you add the things that will be different for your wedding (you might get dressed at church instead of at home, etc.) Make sure your photographer, caterer, baker, florist, and musicians know your time table and that they approve any last minute changes.

Event	Time
1. Rise & Shine/breakfast	
2. Leaving for the ceremony	
3. Photos prior to ceremony	
4. Parents and guests arrive	
5. Ceremony Officially begins	
6. Receiving Line	
7. Wedding Party photos	
8. Leaving for Reception	
9. Arrive at the Reception/Introductions	
10. Toast by Best Man	
11. Celebration Meal	
12. Cake Cutting	
13. Bridal Dance	
14. Dancing	
15. Bride and Groom change clothes	
16. Bride and Groom leave reception	
17. Reception ends	

NOTE: If you are going to change clothes at the reception, make sure someone will take care of the gown and tuxedo.

Giving The Wedding Toast

Generally, the best man serves as the toastmaster, and prepares a list of each person who will be making a toast. There is an established protocol which the couple may or may not choose to follow. You may want to check with the hired musicians for the use of their microphone if the rehearsal or reception is in a very large area and people may have a hard time hearing. You might also consider if the sound system will be set up when you need to speak.

Special Considerations: If you, or someone else, will not be able to stand as you deliver your toast, you may want to make special arrangements ahead of time to move to a location where you will be seen by all.

At The Rehearsal Dinner - You might follow this order:
- The best man toasts the bride
- The bride toasts the groom
- The groom toasts the bride's mother
- The bride's father may toast the groom's parents

During the Reception - You might follow this order:
- The best man toasts the bride and groom
- The groom toasts the bride and her family
- The two fathers toast the bride and groom
- The bride and groom toast each other

Tips for that Perfect Toast
- Don't be long-winded.
- Stand to give a toast; remain seated to receive one.
- Prepare ahead of time; know what you are going to say.
- Mention those you are toasting by name, your relationship to them, and a thought about this wonderful event.
- Add witty anecdotes wherever possible, if they are in good taste and if you can deliver them appropriately
- Speak slowly and loudly enough for all guests to hear.
- You may want to avoid consuming alcohol before your toast.
- Don't forget to cap off the toast with a hearty ending like "Cheers!"